WASHINGTON COUNTY, MARYLAND

# Our Past, Our People

## A HISTORICAL PORTRAIT
### VOLUME II

PUBLISHED BY

# The Herald-Mail Company

JOHN LEAGUE, EDITOR AND PUBLISHER

COPYRIGHT 2005, ALL RIGHTS RESERVED
FIRST EDITION

ISBN: 0-9748853-2-0
PRINTED BY
HBP, INC.
HAGERSTOWN, MD.

Michele

Deb

Dennis

John L.

Susan

Marlene

Brian

Tom

Mindy

Terry

Skip

Andy

Lisa

Linda

John F.

## ACKNOWLEDGMENTS

*The Project Staff*
*Michele Wills, Project Director*
*Dennis Shaw, Book Editor*
*Deb Lanzendorfer, Graphic Design and Layout*
*Susan Snyder, Project Coordinator*
*Brian Sease, Production Coordinator*
*Skip Hutzell, Photo Scanner*
*Tom Crowell, Photo Scanner*
*Andrew (Andy) Schotz, Proofreading*
*Terry Headlee, Proofreading*
*Linda Boward, Sales*

*Washington County Historical Society*
*Melinda (Mindy) Marsden, Executive Director*

*Western Maryland Room —*
*Washington County Free Library*
*John Frye, Historian*

*Corporate Partners*
**Antietam Cable Television, Inc.**
**Washington County Public Schools**
**Callas Contractors, Inc.**
**City of Hagerstown**

*Special Mention*
*Ed Itnyre, Don Corbett, Bill Knode, Larry Yanos*

# The story of "Our Past, Our People"

One day, Herald-Mail Editor and Publisher John League woke up with a vision. "There are so many people in Washington County with incredible stories to tell," he said to himself, even before his first cup of coffee. "I'll bet they have pictures to go with them! I see a book!"

And so it began ...
He took the idea to Marketing Director Michele Wills and said, "Go with it, Michele." And she went with it.
First she assembled a top-notch crew. Former Lifestyle Editor Lisa Tedrick Prejean was the perfect person to edit the book, and Lisa said, "Count me in."
Executive Assistant Susan Snyder, who has a fantastic way with people and with details, lent her charm and her organizational skills to the project, and it was off and running.
"Our Past, Our People," it would be called. It would show local folks doing everyday things, from far back in the 1800s up till 1959.
Next to come on board were the most important people of all – Herald-Mail readers.
"Bring us your photos!," the ads read. And you brought them, big time.
Michele, Susan, Lisa and Assistant to the Publisher Marlene Russell manned the phones and met with folks who brought in their treasured heirloom pictures.
Almost 700 of them were submitted ... wonderful, varied photos showing amazing people doing amazing things, and making history in the process.
Herald-Mail technicians Brian Sease, Skip Hutzell and Tom Crowell set to work on the photos, scanning them into the system to show them at their best.
Then came the hard part – picking which ones to run. Only 200 could fit in the book!
"We'll make it bigger," Michele said. And she did. Now the book could hold nearly 300 photos .... better, although not as many as we wanted. But we did the best we could, and soon the book was almost ready.
We had still more indispensable help. Executive Editor Terry Headlee and reporter Andy Schotz read every single caption. We had outside help with that, too.
John Frye of the Western Maryland Room at Washington County Free Librar, and Mindy Marsden of the Washington County Historical Society also read over every caption, to make sure everything was as accurate as possible.
To them, and to every single person who submitted a photo, we are very, very grateful. It was your book.
But wait! What about all those other photos?
Leave it to Michele. "I've got it!" she said. "Volume II!"
And here you have it, Volume II.
Lisa Tedrick Prejean, alas for us, had taken a full-time job teaching elementary school. And as anyone who has taught elementary school can tell you, the job does not leave time to edit a book. So Michele called Dennis Shaw, a retired Herald-Mail editor and asked him if he'd be willing to fill some very big shoes.
Dennis took one look at Volume I, thought about it for 72 seconds, and said "Yes!"
Michele also hired a graphic designer named Deb Lanzendorfer, who brought a lot of creative design and technical know-how to the project. So, the wheels started spinning again.
The job should have been simpler the second time around, yes? Well ... yes and no.
Some things were easier, thanks to the efforts of everyone involved before. But there was one part that was much, much harder: on top of all the photos we couldn't fit into Volume I, we received 500 more! That made almost 1,000 photos, of which we could run fewer than 300. To make things even harder, we extended the time frame, to include photos from the 1960s in addition to all those other decades.
So, here you have hundreds of wonderful photos submitted by hundreds of readers. We very much hope Volume II is as good as, or maybe even better than, Volume I. That's for you to decide.
Our sincere thanks to you and to everyone who helped make this book possible. Without you, none of this would have been possible.
And keep on keeping on .... Michele woke up one morning and said, "Volume III!"

# On the cover

A popular hangout and meeting place for young people, the Dale St. Store in Hagerstown's West End, drew a crowd from all over Hagerstown from 1960 to 1965.

Morris Miller, who was a regular, remembers there was a dance floor in the back of the store and a jukebox that played the latest hits. The store was run by a couple known as June and Jim. It was open from Monday through Saturday, often as late as 9 or 10 p.m. There was no drinking.

The kids who met there more than 40 years ago still have fond memories of the store. They held a "no class" reunion in 2003 and 130 of them showed up. Two years later, in March 2005, they held another reunion; 145 attended. Another reunion is planned for September 2007. This one will be held at the Potomac Fish and Game Club and is being organized by another Dale Street regular, Vic Hauver of Hagerstown.

Everyone knew the proprietors as June and Jim; and no one could remember their last name. But Morris Miller did some research and came up with the answer: Aldridge.

Dorothy June Kline Aldridge, now 84, is living on South Locust Street in Hagerstown. Her husband, Ellis, more commonly known as Jim, or "Pap," died three years ago. Their photo appears on page 202.

June recalls the days of the Dale St. Store fondly. "They were all good kids," she said. "They loved to dance and, for one dollar the juke box would play dance tunes for a full hour."

This photo was taken by Skip Mason outside the store in 1962. The young men, from left, are: Maurice Dunkin, Ken Henry, Morris Miller, Charles "Jumbo" Mozingo and identical twins Joe and Jay Grumbine.

(Submitted by Christina Sandeen of Boonsboro, daughter of Morris and Linda Miller of Williamsport)

# The Late 1800s

## Kershner's Corner

Joseph I. Kershner operated a broom factory at his grocery store at the northeast corner of North Mulberry Street and East Avenue in Hagerstown. Besides brooms, Kershner sold products that included boots and shoes, confectionery, animal feed, ice cream and fresh oysters. In this 1885 photo, Kershner is standing with his hands on his hips, fourth from the right. None of the assembled neighborhood crowd is identified. The house is still standing.

(Submitted by John McCune of Hagerstown, grandson of Joseph Kershner)

# Track layers

This group of African-American men laid track through Paramount and Reid, north of Hagerstown, for the Western Maryland Rail Road in the 1890s.
(Submitted by Cindy Brezler of Hagerstown)

*Did you know...*

In 1873, the Baltimore and Ohio branch into Hagerstown, known at the time as the Washington County Rail Road, had four trains leaving Hagerstown daily for Weverton and points beyond. Early risers could catch the 5:30 a.m. train which got them to Baltimore at 10:40 a.m. or they could stay aboard and be in Washington by 1:50 p.m.

## Cornet combo

Members of the Keedysville Cornet Band (left) display instruments of varying sizes in this 1865 photo. From right, they are: I.B. Secrist, Jacob Cost, David Bell, Aaron Cost, C.M. Keedy, Alfred Pry, David Kretzer, Samuel Pry, Silas Huffer, A.C. Pry, Josephus Gigeous, William Lantz, Mahlon Knadler, Silas Drener, Emory A. Pry, Alfred Smith, Jacob Eavey, Jacob Keedy, Jacob Lantz and Gen. C. Roher.

(Submitted by Dorothy Ditto Smeins of Dayton, Md.)

## Clear Spring Band

C.A. Hyde (foreground) was the captain of the Clear Spring Band, pictured here on Main Street in the late 1800s.

(Submitted by Larry Gordon of Hagerstown, a cousin of C.A. Hyde)

4

## On the ready

These men with swords crossed and prepared to fight for their country are, from left: Oscar Renner, Martin Gossard and Frank Clayton Nigh. This photo, taken around 1896, was submitted by Richard Nigh of Hagerstown, son of Frank Clayton Nigh.

## The cave of Cavetown

Three adventurous 19th-century spelunkers use a wooden ladder as they prepare to descend into the depths of a cave near Smithsburg in 1877. One of the larger caves in the area, it gave name to the village of Cavetown, a small community east of Hagerstown established in 1815.

Also known as Bushey's Cavern, the cave is next to the railroad tracks off Md. 66 north of its intersection with Md. 64. There is a quarry next to it, which was started in 1881 by George M. Bushey, whose family owned the land. After years of quarry operations nearby, however, "the mountain closed the cave" in 1924, says Peggy Bushey, a great-great-granddaughter of George Bushey.

(Submitted by Mark Trovinger of Sabillasville)

# Old news

The Hagerstown Mail was a weekly newspaper that started in Washington County in 1828. It became a daily newspaper in 1890 and was published in a building on the east side of the first block of Summit Avenue. It was called The Daily Mail by the time it was bought by The Morning Herald in 1920 to become part of The Herald-Mail Company. Editors and compositors of The Hagerstown Mail are shown here in 1891 in the paper's composing room. The compositors are Shawn Socks, Soutty Ludwig, Richard "Dick" Duffey, Mr. Brumer and Mr. Jinkand. The editors are Mrs. Hamilton, Bell and Williams.

(Submitted by Brenda Duffey of Hagerstown, daughter-in-law of Dick Duffey in the photo, probably one of the two young men to the left of the stove pipe. Duffey served as Washington County sheriff from 1919 to 1921 and 1923 to 1926)

## Chewsville family

John Warbel, left, taught at the Mt. Airy School in the 1860s and continued teaching for the next two decades. This photograph was taken at the Warbel home on Bovey Road in Chewsville in 1898. John's nephew, Henry Warbel, is holding the horse at right. Next to Henry is his wife, Nettie Gray Warbel. Beside her, with the baby buggy, is Grace Warbel. The other child is unidentified. John Warbel died in 1904 and is buried in the Beaver Creek Lutheran Cemetery. He lost his right arm when he was a youth. The arm is said to be buried in the Kieffer Funk Cemetery east of Hagerstown.

(Submitted by Connie Leisinger of Chewsville, granddaughter of Henry and Grace Warbel)

# Riding high

The Hagerstown Bicycle Club was organized in Hagerstown in 1884 with 14 members. The club held races which included the 1-mile dash, the 2-mile lap race and the 2-mile handicap. The photobelow, taken in 1888, shows club member Chester Hays and his bicycle known as "The Wheel." Hays was a member of the family that owned R.M. Hays & Bros. Stationery at 28 W. Washington St. in Hagerstown. In the 1890s, the store sold books, stationery, wallpaper, window shades and curtain poles. It remained in operation there until the 1970s.

Chester Hays might have been riding this bicycle in August of 1891, when, according to a local news report, "while riding his bicycle near Mechanicstown (Thurmont), he ran over a large rattlesnake which was coiled directly in his path. The wheel passed over the back of the snake which made a strike at Mr. Hays as he flashed by but it failed to strike him."

(Submitted by the Washington County Historical Society)

## Did you know...

In 1870 the first all-metal bicycle appeared. The pedals were still atttached directly to the front wheel with no free-wheeling mechanism. You would purchase a wheel as large as your leg length would allow.

This machine was the first one to be called a bicycle ("two wheel"). These bicycles enjoyed a great popularity among young men of means (they cost an average worker six months' pay), with the heyday being the decade of the 1880s.

# The wheels are coming

The League of American Wheelmen, bicyclists on their high-wheelers, ride down North Potomac Street in to Hagerstown's Public Square in July 1889. (Submitted by the Hagerstown Roundhouse Museum)

# Keedys
## of Keedysville

Clementine Keedy Eavey looks down from the balcony of her house on Main Street in Keedysville in 1887. She and her husband, Jacob E. Eavey, ran a store on the first floor of the house. The folks standing in front of the store are unidentified.

Clementine was the daughter of Christian and Mary Ellen Carr Keedy. Christian Keedy was engaged in the lumber, grain, coal and banking businesses and in 1872 became the first mayor of the town.

(Submitted by Dorothy Ditto Smeins of Dayton, Md.)

# Basket Ball

From 1853 until 1912, female students attended a seminary founded by the Lutheran Church on what is now the site of Washington County Hospital in Hagerstown. Here they're taking a break to play "Basket Ball," although the hoops can't be seen. This photo is from an antique postcard submitted by Rose Marie Suders of Hagerstown.

Basket Ball,
Kee-Mar College,
Hagerstown, Md.

# Beaver Creek

John S. Rohrer and Florence Landis Rohrer, seated at center in the photo at left, assembled their family around 1890 for a portrait that included, from left: Elva Rohrer, Frank Rohrer, Ira Rohrer, Maude Rohrer Hagerman, Carrie Rohrer Stine, Clayton Rohrer, and, standing next to his father, John D. Rohrer. John S. Rohrer was a farmer in the Beaver Creek area. Sons Frank and Ira Rohrer went into business together as Rohrer Brothers, selling farm machinery on West Antietam Street in Hagerstown.

(Photo submitted by Veronica Ludwig of Hagerstown, daughter of Frank Rohrer)

# German immigrants

Jacob John Schlotterbeck and his wife, Kathrina Schmidt Schlotterbeck, join their children for this 1880s photo taken in their stone house, which is still standing next to what is now Cedar Lawn Cemetery west of Hagerstown. Jacob and Kathrina came to Washington County from Wurttemberg, Germany. They are seated here on either side of Jacob John Jr. Behind them, from left, are George Albert Schlotterbeck, Bertha Schlotterbeck Heimel, John Daniel Schlotterbeck, William Schlotterbeck and Charles Schlotterbeck.

(Photo submitted by Larry Schlotterbeck of Falling Waters, W.Va., great-grandson of George Albert Schlotterbeck)

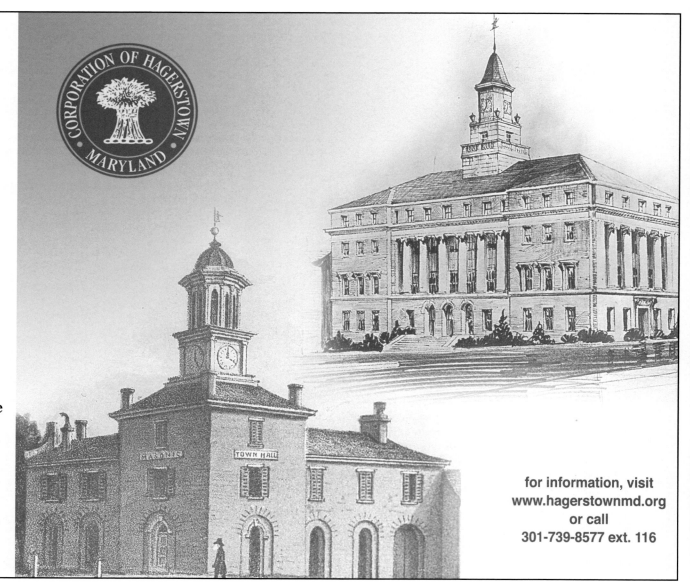

Since 1762,
the City of
Hagerstown,
in partnership with
the community,
has been providing
superior services...

... to make the city
the location of choice
for residents,
businesses
and visitors.

for information, visit
www.hagerstownmd.org
or call
301-739-8577 ext. 116

*Washington County Public Schools*
*Celebrating 140 years of commitment*
*to public education in Washington County*

## Ensuring world-class
## education for all students

# Waiting for mail

Two unidentified gentlemen keep warm while waiting for mail at the Reid Station post office north of Hagerstown, probably in the 1890s. The post office closed in 1907. David Horst was the first postmaster.

(Submitted by Cindy Brezler of Hagerstown)

## Did you know...

The postage stamp was introduced in the United States in 1840. In 1845, Congress reduced and regularized postal rates with a uniform rate of 5¢ for distances under 300 miles.

## Did you know...

Thomas Alva Edison announced his invention of the first phonograph, a device for recording and replaying sound, on Nov. 21, 1877, and he demonstrated the device for the first time on Nov. 29 (he patented it on Feb. 19, 1878).

# Baxter Store

A general store run by D.T. Baxter stood at 81-83 Main St. in Hancock, at the site now occupied by Petals 'n' Bows. It is not known if Mr. Baxter is the gentleman in the photo, which was taken in the late 1890s. The child is also unidentified.

(Submitted by the Hancock Historical Society)

# The 1900s

## Get it at Creager's

The H.L. Creager store stood on Main Street in Hancock. The popular store, pictured here in the early 1900s, sold just about everything. There were several stores of this type on Main Street. No one in the photo is identified, though it is known that Mr. Creager isn't in it. The building is still standing today and is used for storage by the owner, Harry Barker.

(Submitted by the Hancock Historical Society)

## Trovinger Mill

The milling of grain was the first major industry in Washington County, and many mills sprang up along the county's waterways in the 18th and 19th centuries. Jacob Rohrer's mill was built in 1771 on Antietam Creek, three miles east of Hagerstown. Made of fieldstone, it is one of the few mills that remain today. When this photo was taken around 1900, the mill belonged to Joseph Trovinger. It had come to be known as Trovinger Mill and was, appropriately enough, on Trovinger Mill Road. It was placed on the National Register of Historic Places in 1975.

(Submitted by Mark Trovinger of Sabillasville, Md. Historical information from "Architectural and Historical Treasures of Washington County, Maryland" by Pat Schooley)

## Blind to adversity

Rosie Baker was a blind child who lived at 123 N. Cannon Ave. in Hagerstown most of her life. Born blind in 1897, she was one of six children born to John and Beada Harbaugh Baker. Her father worked as a desk clerk at night at the Maryland Hotel in Hagerstown. He died at 42. Beada couldn't cope with having six children and taking care of a blind child, and ended up in an asylum.

Rosie's oldest sister, Agnes Theresa "Clazzie" Baker, came to the rescue, taking care of the entire family. Clazzie worked at the Hagerstown Shoe Factory. Before she left for work in the morning, she would pack Rosie's lunch and leave it on the kitchen table in a bowl so Rosie would know where to find it.

As Rosie got older, she made daily train trips to a school for the blind in Baltimore. She could tell you every stop the train made and which town it was in. She even offered directions to passengers who needed help. She filled her evenings playing the piano, knitting and teaching those skills to her cousins. Clazzie never married, as she felt nobody would want to marry a woman with a ready-made family. Her commitment to her siblings never wavered and she cared for Rosie until she had a stroke and was unable to continue. Clazzie died in 1956. Her niece, Dorothy Brandenburg, took in Rosie until Rosie went to live at the Fahrney-Keedy nursing home near Boonsboro. Rosie continued to keep busy during her days there, and if dementia patients got lost in the hall, she would lead them back to their rooms. She died in 1968 at age 72 and is buried at Rose Hill Cemetery in Hagerstown.

The two older photos were taken around 1903. The one at the left is of Rosie; the other (top right) is of Clazzie, left, and their sister Mary. The later photo, taken in 1952, shows Rosie, right, Clazzie, and their great-nephew Lee, son of Dorothy Brandenburg.

(Photos and history provided by Barbara Reeder of Boonsboro, great-niece of Rosie and Clazzie)

# *A* cool one

Brothers Charles and Jim Lushbaugh ran Lushbaugh's Saloon about 100 years ago at the corner of Elizabeth and Leroy streets in Hagerstown's West End. Charles is at center in this photo taken in the early 1900s; Jim is at right. The man at left is unidentified.

(Submitted by Margaret Richards of Hagerstown, granddaughter of Charles Lushbaugh)

## Upping block

Taken around 1900, the photo at right shows the northeast corner of the square in Smithsburg. The gentleman pictured is probably L. B. Brenner, standing in front of his general store where the Dixie Eatery stands now. Brenner is working on an "upping block," which offered a place to step in order to get on your horse, according to Charlie Slick, president of the Smithsburg Historical Society, who submitted this photo. At various times, Mr. Brenner's general store stood on three of the four corners of the square. It was in operation into the 1920s.

## Meat cutters

Several members of the Sigler family of Smithsburg were meat cutters, and Michael Sigler brandishes his knife and sharpening steel to show his profession in this 1902 photo. Beside the bearded Mr. Sigler is his wife, Margaret Ridenour Sigler. Standing at center in the back is their son, Charles Henderson Sigler. To the right of him is his wife, Catherine Elenora Gilbert Sigler. The young boy at center is C. Gilbert Sigler. The others are unidentified.

(Submitted by the Smithsburg Historical Society)

## Going courting

Frank Spielman, 21, of Hagerstown tried to impress Meda A. Storm of Tilghmanton by taking her out in a fashionable horse and buggy while courting her in 1902. It must have worked, for four years later they married and settled in Hagerstown.

(Submitted by George B. Spielman of Hagerstown, great-nephew of Frank and Meda Spielman)

## Geetings

In photo at left, W. C. Geeting, owner and operator of the Keedysville Milling Company in Keedysville, is joined by his wife, Ada Huffer Geeting; their 7-year-old son, Russell; and their 3-year-old daughter, Rachel, in this 1903 family portrait.
(Submitted by Elaine Strausner of Middletown, granddaughter of W.C. Geeting)

*Did you know...*

**Talking machines advertised**

The Reliable Furniture Company at 17 W. Franklin St., "next to Oak Spring," advertised in 1905: "Talking machines and phonographs on easy payment. Never before has there been such an offer made to the music-loving public of Hagerstown and vicinity. Only $1 down and $1 per week on any talking machine or phonograph. We have them in prices ranging from $10 to $45. A large selection of disc and cylinder records."

## Millers

Mr. and Mrs. D. Frank Miller (photo at right) had five children when this photo was taken between 1905 and 1907 on their Keedysville farm. Downey is standing in back; Hazel is on her father's knee; Nell is being held by her mother; Mary is standing beside her mother; and Jess is in front. Sisters Kathryn and Ruth later joined the family.
(Submitted by Nancy Kneisley Costain of Arlington, Va., daughter of Mary Miller Kneisley)

# The Williamsport School

Omer Kaylor, who taught fourth grade at the Williamsport School, stands outside with the class of 1902. An old list of names identifies the students, though some names are difficult to make out. The list appears to be, from left:

FRONT ROW: Maria Curfman, Sallie Wine, Mary Miller, Alice Chrisman, Sallie Maderon, Geraldine Turner, Joseph Weederhall, Dwight Wagoner, Arthur Knodle, Eli Beachley and Frank Stevens.

MIDDLE ROW: Bertha Corby, Bertha Chrisman, Anne Snyder, Susie McKalvey, May Richter, Lina Kelly, Ada McElroy, William Hetzer, William Templeton, Paul Miller and William Sterling.

BACK ROW: John Forsythe, Harry Hetzer, John Ditlow, Forsythe, John Turner, Coulter Hewitt and Lynch.

(Submitted by Robert Young of Hagerstown, grandson of Alice Chrisman)

## Monument to history

Union and Confederate Civil War veterans gather at Antietam Battlefield in a photo believed to have been taken on Oct. 13, 1903. The likely occasion was the dedication of the William McKinley monument, which stands near the Burnside Bridge parking lot. In this photo, taken by C.H. Petcher, Union veterans are standing in the back row and Confederate veterans are seated in front. The tall man third from the right in the back row is Gen. A. Carman, who was caretaker of the National Cemetery in Sharpsburg at the time. Carman joined the Army at the same time as William McKinley, who served at Antietam and went on to become president of the United States. McKinley was assassinated on Sept. 14, 1901.

A handwritten caption on the back of the photo reads: "The Gray Lovingly Surrounded by the Blue on Antietam battlefield." The photo was submitted by Marcia Swain of Hagerstown, who inherited it from her grandmother, Inez Smith Swain, who lived in Sharpsburg. Marcia Swain says her grandmother, who died in 1966, "talked about the Civil War like it had just happened."

# Help is on the way

Lowman's Ambulance in Hagerstown had a two-horsepower engine at the ready to rush victims to the hospital in the early part of the last century. The owner was Keller Lowman, and the driver here is John H. Rohrer.
(Submitted by Dave White of Hagerstown)

*Did you know...*

In 1903, an article in The Daily Mail newspaper read, "While driving in the vicinity of Jonathan and Franklin streets last night, Edgar S. Smith, of North Potomac Street, narrowly escaped being run down by an automobile. Fortunately he had perfect control of his horse and drew the animal to one side of the street just as the machine whizzed by."

# Leitersburg, 1909

Edward C. Weigand – the tall one at the back – was the teacher at the Leitersburg School in 1909. Among his students was his daughter, Mary Irene, who's at the right end of the middle row. Next to her is Charlotte Strite. The girl third from left in the middle row, with the braid over her shoulder, is Jessie Snodderly. The others are unidentified.
(Submitted by Maurice F. Johnston of Hagerstown, son of Mary Irene Weigand and grandson of Edward C. Weigand)

# At work on time

George Franklin Baker stands behind the counter of his jewelry store at 24 E. Washington St. in Hagerstown, sometime in the first decade of the 20th century.

Baker, from the Downsville area, didn't own a car or drive before he opened the store, according to his granddaughter, Rose Hurd of Hagerstown, who submitted this photo. Instead, he pedaled around the county on a bicycle, stopping at farms to repair clocks and sell watches and jewelry to the ladies.

Baker was the official time inspector for the Western Maryland and B&O railroads. Railroad employees brought their watches in to be certified for accuracy. He was required to keep a log of the watches checked, along with names and dates.

He taught his daughter-in-law how to repair clocks and string pearls. Later on, he hired a watchmaker named Mr. Smartz, who remained with him until he retired.

Baker's Jewelry Store moved to 32 E. Washington St. in 1912 and stayed there until it closed in 1962.

# Dressed to go

After Dr. Victor D. Miller married Nellie B. Loose on June 1, 1905, the wedding party went outside to pose for a photo. But the photographer was late, and the bridal couple had to catch a train out of town, so they changed into their traveling clothes before he arrived.

The photo was taken on South Prospect Street in Hagerstown in the yard between the two Loose houses, which were between the Women's Club and the Dry Bridge. The wedding was held at the Presbyterian Church, one block away.

In the photo, the bride and groom are seated at center in dark clothing. To the left of the groom are Alex Armstrong and Mary Miller, sister of the groom; to the right of the bride are Margaret Neil and Jess McLanahan Nelson. Standing behind them, from

left, are Grace Loose, Dr. Preston Miller, Anna Loose, three unidentified men, Margaret Loose, Rose Loose, Louise Hewitt, Sam Loose and J. Pearson Loose. Others known to have been in the wedding party are Alpheus Beall, James L. Norris Jr., Alexander Lane and Clarence L. Keedy. The dog's name is Saltrum.

(Submitted by Col. Henry Miller of Hagerstown, son of the bride and groom)

# Among friends

   Like a young lady of any era, Cora Strite Troup liked to invite friends over for a good time. This photo, taken around 1905, captures a light moment during one such get-together. The setting is probably the parlor or living room of Cora's house at 52 Broadway in Hagerstown. Cora is seated on the floor at right, in the fanned white dress. None of her friends is identified. (Submitted by Barbara Hoover of Hagerstown, granddaughter of Cora Strite Troup)

## Digging in

Jacob Roessner (holding shovel in photo below) was a charter member of Trinity Lutheran Church in Hagerstown when it was built on West Franklin Street in 1868. Forty-one years later, a new church was built at the corner of Randolph Avenue and Potomac Street. Roessner was asked to dig the first shovelful of dirt at the groundbreaking on June 14, 1909. Behind Roessner on a wooden walkway is Dr. Jacob S. Simon, reading Scripture from the Bible. Simon was pastor of the church for 38 years, from 1902 to 1940. In the background is a house on Randolph Street.

(Submitted by Trinity Lutheran Church)

## The reverend's visit

Rev. Charles Jared Curtis, rector of both the Sharpsburg and Lappans Episcopal churches, pays a visit to the home of William and Emma Grove Blackford in Sharpsburg sometime between 1905 and 1910. The above photo was taken in front of the Blackfords' home, close to the national cemetery. Standing, from left, are Arthur Yancey, Rev. Curtis, Robert Yancey and William Franklin Blackford. Seated, from left, are Emma Grove Blackford; Pauline Blackford, the daughter of William and Emma; Rev. Curtis' wife, Mary; and Jeanette Grove, Emma's sister. The Yancey brothers were family friends.

William Blackford was a partner in a grocery store on the square in Sharpsburg near where Nutter's Ice Cream store is today. His father was Col. John Blackford, who owned the Ferry Hill farm in Maryland, overlooking the Potomac River. Emma was well known for her baked "beatin biscuits," and for her piano rendition of "Maryland, My Maryland."

(Submitted by Wilson Blackford Waddy of Williamsport, grandson of William and Emma Grove Blackford)

# The 1910s

## Coal's here

Charles Rhimes, left, and Frank A. Spielman deliver coal in Hagerstown in 1912. They worked for John W. Rohrer. (Submitted by George B. Spielman of Sharpsburg, great-nephew of Frank Spielman)

*Did you know...*

In 1857, coal was replacing wood as the favored source of heat. Godfrey Goetz of Greencastle offered coal stoves for prices from $24 to $48 and "parlor furnaces" for $45 to $60.

## If the shoe fits

Frank W. Nield was 20 and his wife, Margaret, was 18 in 1913 when their photos were taken in Hagerstown. Five years later, Frank started repairing shoes in a shed next to his home. In 1927, he moved the operation to Howard and Chestnut streets and built what he called "The Largest Ladies Shoe in the World" to attract passers-by to Nield's Shoe Repair. Nield retired in 1945 due to poor health, but the business continued for another five years. The 10-foot shoe, which once was dismantled and displayed in the annual Alsatia Mummers Parade, was torn down in 1952.

(Photos submitted by Julie Shaffer Funk of Hagerstown, granddaughter of Frank and Margaret Nield)

## A clean sweep

Two street cleaners appear very well dressed as they as they negotiate trolley tracks in front of Trinity Lutheran Church on North Potomac Street in Hagerstown. Their truck's solid tires, chain drive and front put it in the years between 1915 and 1920. (Submitted by Dave White of Hagerstown)

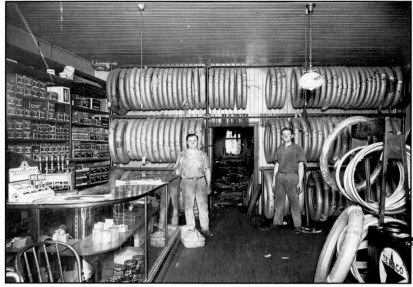

## Tired out

Maurice Domenici Sr., left, and his son, Maurice "Jack" Domenici Jr., pause from work in the Domenici Tire Company at 163 S. Potomac St. in Hagerstown around 1914.

Maurice Sr. came to the U.S. from Italy in 1881 and moved to Hagerstown from Washington, D.C., with the Crawford Bicycle Works. He went with Crawford when it moved to Connecticut, but returned to Hagerstown in 1909 and opened his tire vulcanizing shop at 328 S. Potomac St. In 1914, he moved it into the building at the northwest corner of South Potomac and Antietam streets which still bears the Domenici name in relief over the door.

(Photo submitted by Adeline Domenici of Leitersburg, whose husband, the late Maurice Richard Domenici, was the grandson of Maurice Domenici Sr. and worked at the tire company until it closed in 1960)

## On time

General Timekeeper I. J. Holliday was assisted by G. N. Buzzard, G. J. Fritts and W. C. Metz in the timekeeper's office of the Western Maryland Railway on Dec. 18, 1913. The office was located in the Western Maryland Station on Burhans Boulevard. (Submitted by Dave White of Hagerstown)

# Yard gang

Charles Vernon "C. V." Stone in photo at right (center) stands next to Engine No. 10, a "switcher" built around 1890 to move rail cars around in the yards. The photo was taken on Western Maryland Railway property around 1910, near where the Hagerstown Roundhouse Museum stands today.

To the left of C.V. Stone is his brother, Oscar Stone. The other men are unidentified. After a rail strike, C.V. Stone left the business and opened a barber shop, Stone's Barber and Beauty Shop, at 614 W. Washington St. in Hagerstown. It was in operation from the mid 1920s to the early 1930s, when it moved to the third block of South Potomac Street.

(Submitted by Freda Stone of Hagerstown, daughter-in-law of Charles Vernon "C. V." Stone)

## Did you know...

In the early 1900s, Hagerstown was becoming a railroad center, with a network of tracks meeting near the center of town, which would eventually cause it to be nicknamed the Hub City.

# Test driver

Mr. and Mrs. George Taylor put their son, Wallace, behind the wheel of their Hudson on a wintry day in 1916 on Conococheague Street in Williamsport.

(Submitted by the Williamsport Town Museum)

# Mexican War fever

Hagerstown's Company B heads off to fight in the Mexican War on June 21, 1916. Alerted only the day before, the civilian soldiers left shortly after 8 a.m. on two coaches from the B&O Station at Summit Avenue and Antietam Street, where The Herald-Mail now stands.

A crowd estimated at 3,000 was on hand to watch the departure and the parade around downtown which preceded it. The parade was led by the Municipal Band and included the local Boy Scout drum and bugle corps.

The Daily Mail newspaper of the day reported that: "Patriotism ran riot, yet withal the crowd was most orderly and observant. People of all classes mingled together in the true American spirit."

Col. Charles A. Little, commander of the First Maryland Regiment, left with Company B. Included in his staff was Capt. William Preston Lane Jr., adjutant of the First Regiment. Lane, a Hagerstown native, later served in France with the 115th Infantry, and as governor of Maryland from 1947 to 1951.

Civilians in Hagerstown organized a drive for funds to aid families who were left without incomes when their breadwinners answered the call to arms to serve on the Mexican front. The militiamen went to a training camp set up at Laurel, Md., for Maryland National Guard units. They were there only a few days before leaving for duty along the Mexican border at Eagle Pass, Texas.

The U.S. sent troops to the Mexican border before formally entering World War I. The Germans were attempting to stir up trouble there so the U.S. would be diverted from possible support of the Allied forces in Europe. Congress declared war on Germany on April 2, 1917, after the infamous "Zimmerman Telegram" was intercepted. In it, Germany asked Mexico to join it in the war. In exchange, Germany promised to help Mexico regain territory in Texas, Arizona and New Mexico.

(Photo provided by The Herald-Mail. Historical background from The Daily Mail newspaper of June 21, 1956. Hagerstown's old Post Office building on Summit Avenue can be seen in the upper right corner of this photo. Still standing today, it houses Community Action Council. Next to it is the fire hall which still houses the Antietam Volunteer Fire Company.)

## Music man

C. Edward Heard, the man in the back at the center with the moustache, was leader of the Washington County High School Orchestra when this photo was taken in 1917. A musician at heart, he was also choir director at Zion Reformed Church in Hagerstown. Prior to 1915, he also organized the Silverine Band, the forerunner of the Hagerstown Municipal Band.

Heard was a businessman by profession, part owner of Boyer & Heard on West Franklin Street in Hagerstown, a flour mill where oats, hay and coal were sold. In the early 1930s, he was a judge of the Orphan's Court, and later became a police magistrate.

Second from the right in the photo, with trombone, is C. Edward Heard's son, Harold Albert Heard Sr. The other musicians are unidentified.

(Submitted by Peggie Marie Heard Roscoe of Hagerstown, granddaughter of C. Edward Heard and daughter of Harold Albert Heard Sr.)

## Band on the move

Members of the Boonsboro Band rode in a large open bandwagon pulled by four horses to get to their engagements. The wagon had seats laid out like those in a bus. The players would meet at the square in Boonsboro and play several numbers before going to perform at various picnics. This photo was taken at the annual Redmen's picnic grounds near Keedsyville between 1917 and 1920. From left, the band members are: Charles Ford, George Ford, Charles Huffer, unidentified, Polk Itnyre, Earl Glenn, unidentified, unidentified, unidentified, Charles Koogle, Calvin Flook, Hurley Herr, Elsworth Ford, Lemuel Cline, Vincent Flook and another Mr. Flook.

The photo was submitted by B.J. Morgan of Keedysville, whose father, Leon Morgan, remembered hearing the band play in Boonsboro. B.J. Morgan says its music was "a really big thing" back in those days. "You couldn't just pop in a cassette," he says. "There weren't a lot of other opportunities to hear music played."

## Clear start

Students at Clear Spring High School, classes of 1916 to 1918, pose for a photo not long after the school opened in 1915. From left, they are: FRONT ROW: Cornelius Snyder, Kieffer Seibert, William Gardner, Francis Smith, Prather Perry, Roman Gehr, Joe Forsythe and Walter Peterman. SECOND ROW: Louise Seibert, Eldon Hawbaker, Miriam Powers, Laura Roach and Maggie Kelley. THIRD ROW: Daisy Rowland, Elaine Foster, Kate Herbert, Milbry Schnebly, Catharine Grosh, Ada Gossard, Pearl Funkhouser, Mary Shircliffe, Cathryn Schnebly, Lillie McDonald, Frances Hollinger, Mary Corbett, Mary Repp, Nellie Newkirk and Joseph Shook. FOURTH ROW: School principal George Sites, Christine Rowland, Bessie Snyder, Pauline McKalvey, Martha Bartles, Vera Schnebly, Anna Moore and Louise Boward. TOP ROW: Billy Deiht, Harold Snyder, Clarence Funkhouser and Helen Schnebly.

This photo was submitted by Jim and Anne Seibert of Clear Spring. Jim Seibert is a grandson of Kieffer Seibert, in the photo. The Seiberts acquired the photo at a yard sale, but none of the people was identified. At a reunion banquet of the school's alumni association, they ran into Nora Snyder, then in her 90s. She was a 1925 graduate of the school, and later she was Jim Seibert's teacher in the Clear Spring Elementary School. She later became principal of the school. The Seiberts asked her if she could identify the students in the photo, and without hesitation, she provided the names and eventual marital status of everyone in it. (Photo of Nora Snyder is a Herald-Mail file photo)

# Long Ridge Sunday School

Members of the Long Ridge Sunday School in 1915 included, from left: BACK ROW: Mary Virginia "Jennie" Cooper, D.W. Cooper, Lillian Clevenger, Ada McCusker, Jesselene Clevenger, Alma Cooper, Bessie Exline, Ethel Munson, Mary Cooper, Bertie Hill, Rita Cooper and Charlie Mort THIRD ROW: Ross Lee, Raymond McCusker, Marshall McCusker, Ernest Mort, Austin McCusker, Raymond Mort, Albert McCusker and Elmer McCusker SECOND ROW: Merle Clevenger, Margurite Clevenger, Alfereta Hixon, O'rintha Zies, Etta Exline, Theodore Cooper, Allen McCusker, Jesse McCusker, Ross Rishop and Earl Munson FRONT ROW: Rosalie Exline, Louise Exline, Theodore Barnhart, Ethel Exline, Wyona McCusker, Olive Barnhart, Lester McCusker, Edwin Cooper, Agatha Zies and Martha Zies.

The Sunday School was on Woodmont Road west of Hancock. The building was originally a community center, but with the church so far away, it was used for the Sunday School.

(Submitted by Nancy Hofe of Martinsburg, W.Va., granddaughter of Mary Virginia "Jennie" and D.W. Cooper and daughter of Edwin Cooper and Agatha Zies)

# Hopewell hopefuls

Teacher Vera Faulders, the tallest person in the photo, stands outside the Hopewell School around 1919 behind the 29 students who kept her busy teaching all seven grades, K-6, at the one-room schoolhouse. Closed down in the 1930s, the school stood on the west side of Hopewell Road just south of Washington Street west of Hagerstown. A private home now stands on the site. Seated on the ground, from left, are: Mark Hamby, Paul Harsh, Ruth Smith, Harry Doub, Robert Koontz, Paul Shank, unidentified. MIDDLE ROW: Edward Cushen, Blanche Smith, Frank Hamby, Elizabeth Harsh, Nancy Kershner, Eugene Kershner, unidentified, Mary Ambrose, LeRoy Wiles, Sam Ditto. TOP ROW: Emmert Doub, Helen Winger, Edgar Shank, Harriet Doub, Howard Ditto, Mary Bair, George Harsh, Anna Bair, Lloyd Harsh, Robert Beckley, Sarah Bartles, William Ambrose.

(Submitted by Paul Shank of Hagerstown, who is seated on the ground in the photo, second from right)

## Donkey business

Susan Regina Martin gets a supporting hand from her sister, Pearl Martin, as she sits astride a donkey in front of the Alsatia Club on West Washington Street in Hagerstown around 1910. The sisters lived in the Wareham Building across the street. Their mother was a housekeeper for local physicians.

(Submitted by Margaret Kline of Hagerstown, granddaughter of Susan Regina Martin)

### Did you know...

On April 10, 1912, the RMS Titanic set sail from Southampton on her maiden voyage to New York. At that time, she was the largest and most luxurious ship ever built and was referred to as being unsinkable.

At 11:40 p.m. on April 14, 1912, she struck an iceberg. Less than three hours later, the Titanic sank below the waves, taking more than 1,500 passengers and crew down with her.

Of the 1,324 passengers and 899 crew members on board at the time, only 706 were saved.

## Enjoying the sun

Catherine Kimler, wife of a well-known potter, Joseph Kimler, sits outside her house at 26 E. Water St. in Smithsburg in 1918.

(Submitted by Mark Trovinger of Sabillasville, Md.)

## Kenny Coffee

William Palmer, Walter Glesner and Lester Trovinger (left to right) await customers in the C.D. Kenny Coffee, Tea and Spice Shop at 18 N. Potomac St. in Hagerstown in 1915.
(Submitted by Mark Trovinger of Sabillasville, a cousin of Lester Trovinger)

## Meat market

The Harsh Meat Market was a familiar fact of life in Williamsport for more than a century – if you knew where to look. Albert "Butch" Harsh started the business in 1890 on Artizan Street. Later he moved it to Conococheague Street, then to Potomac Street, then to another location on the same street, 5 E. Potomac, where it stayed until 1959. In 1947, his son, Martin "Bud" Harsh Sr., took over the business, and after his father died, he returned it to its roots, constructing a new building for it at the same site on Artizan Street where it began. His son, Martin "Buck" Harsh Jr., was on board by then, and he kept the business going until 1988, when he sold the retail side to an employee, but kept the slaughterhouse operating until 2004. The photo, taken in 1918, shows Albert Harsh and one of his children in front of the original market on Artizan Street. (Submitted by Martin "Buck" and Betty Harsh of Williamsport)

## Machinists on parade

The International Association of Machinists Union, Black Rock Lodge No. 557, takes part in a 1917 Labor Day parade on West Washington Street in Hagerstown. Leroy V. Crist is third from the left. The others are unidentified.

(Submitted by L. Victor Crist of Hagerstown, son of Leroy V. Crist)

## Star quality

Frank Burnett, at the helm, put in a plug for Star Brand shoes when he decked up his horses and wagon to participate in Hancock's annual parade in 1914. Standing just behind him is Ada Dobson Gunnels. The other riders, from left, are Rosalie Sagle Rankin, Isabelle Creagar Snead (barely visible), Martha Creagar Snead, Julia Rankin, Verna Dobson; Lucille Widmyer Creagar, Elsie Huber Rash and, standing in a white top hat, Tom Gilleece. The two women seated at the right may be a Ms. Ditto and a Ms. Ankenney.

The photo was taken on High Street in Hancock. Tom Gilleece and Frank T. Mason sold the above-mentioned shoes in what became the Cornelius Furniture Store on Main Street, the current location of Douglas Motors.

(Submitted by the Hancock Historical Society)

## Jordan Road family

Robert Howard Reichard Sr. and his wife Otelia raised three children on Arch Spring Farm off Jordan Road near Downsville. Pictured around 1915, the family consisted of, from left: R. Howard Reichard Jr. Otelia Rowland Reichard, J. Rowland Reichard, Robert Howard Reichard Sr., and Ruth Reichard. J. Rowland Reichard was a minister at Manor Church of the Brethren for 47 years.

(Submitted by Judy Reichard of Falling Waters, W.Va., daughter-in-law of J. Rowland Reichard)

### *Did you know...*

**Typhoid fever blamed on water**

The County Board of Health released a report published in the March 16, 1915, Daily Mail blamed bad water supplies for the prevalence of typhoid in rural areas and small towns where three-fifths of Washington County's population lived. "The milk test made August 1914, in Hagerstown, showed that the people were not getting just what they had paid for."

## Well, well

Elsie Martz Winders sits next to the wooden water pump by the well at her home on Cool Hollow Road in Beaver Creek around 1918. The pump is gone, but the well is still providing water with the help of an electric pump.

(Submitted by Virginia Martin of Hagerstown, daughter of Elsie Martz Winders)

# Cocktail party

A Sunday afternoon cocktail party was held in 1916 or 1917 at the rear of the Miller House, 135 W. Washington St. in Hagerstown. The partygoers, from left, were:

STANDING: Nellie L. Miller, Anna Jamison, Mrs. Wilbur "Kit" Bridges, Lou Huyett, Grace Loose, Etta Loose and, partly hidden, Helen Bower. The bald head behind Helen Bower belongs to her husband, John Bower. Continuing from left are Vincent Jamison, Harry Keedy and Jeni McKee.

KNEELING AND SITTING ON THE GRASS: Lydia Edwards Cuntz holding her daughter, whose name we don't know; Henry L. Miller, later Col. Miller; Dr. Victor D. Miller; Max Huyett and Don McKee.

(Submitted by Col. Henry L. Miller of Hagerstown, the only member of the party still living)

## High tea

Well-dressed guests enjoy an outdoor tea party at the home of Jennie Witter, center, on Potomac Street in Boonsboro on a Sunday in 1910.
(Submitted by Doug Bast of Boonsboro)

## Wolfingers united

The Wolfinger clan gathers for a reunion in 1912, starting a tradition that has continued for more than 90 years to the present day. They're seated in front of the 1850s house at the family's dairy farm on Lehman's Mill Road. The little girl at lower left is Lillian Hartman Brown. Three back from her (wearing dark jacket) is Daniel Boward, and behind him is Samuel E. Hartman. At front right side is Clarence Wolfinger. The woman three back from him beside the child is Bertha Wolfinger Boward, Daniel Boward's wife.

(Submitted by Ed Beeler of Waynesboro, Pa. The Wolfingers are relatives on his mother's side of the family)

## Four Locks berth

A canal boat (lower right) sits in drydock on the berm side of Lock 47 at Four Locks on the Potomac River around 1910. Samuel Fernsner, at right in the lineup of three men, repaired canal boats there, and also operated the Snyder-Fernsner Store seen at the upper right. Standing next to him is his son, Paul Richard. The other man is unidentified.

(Photo submitted by Paul Gantz of Hagerstown. Historical information from Cracker Barrel Magazine, June/July 2003)

# Berry picking

Joe Brown's raspberry patch in Mousetown, near Boonsboro, kept the family busy at harvest time in 1910. Among the crew here are probably Joe's wife and their daughter Vada. Children worked early in the day, under adult supervision, to make sure they "picked them clean."
(Submitted by Doug Bast of Boonsboro)

## A home to many

Since 1900, four families have lived in this house on Black Rock Road near Beaver Creek, on a stretch now known as Meadowrock Drive. The house still stands, and was recently purchased by William and Patricia Riggle. When this photo was taken around 1912, it was occupied by the Lung family, but last names were changing as children got married, as evidenced by the line-up here.

From left:

BACK ROW: Tom Summers, Charlie Summers, Clegg Lung, Annie Summers, Florence Welty, Geneva Summers, Luther Lung and Effie Lung

MIDDLE ROW: Grace Summers, Alice Summers, Charles Martin, Alvey Lung and George Crouse

FRONT ROW: John Lung, John Summers, Amelia Lung, Carrie Martin holding Guy Martin, and Mazie Lung Crouse holding Vernon Crouse

(Submitted by E. Richard Martin and Patricia C. Martin of Hagerstown. E. Richard Martin is the grandson of Charles and Carrie Martin in the photo)

## A Gray day

A large number of the descendants of Peter Gray, of Beaver Creek, assembled in 1915 for a reunion. They met at the home of Mr. and Mrs. Henry W. Gray on the Leitersburg Pike. A luncheon was served in the large orchard.

Those present were: Mr. and Mrs. Henry W. Gray; Mrs. Mollie Shilling and her daughter, Edna; Mr. and Mrs. Guy Shilling and their daughter; Mr. and Mrs. Sylvester Ramsey of Hagerstown; Mrs. William Ramsey of Hagerstown and her children; Mr. and Mrs. John W. Albert of State Line, Pa., and their children, Mary and Ray; Mr. and Mrs. Charles Dietrich of Fairview and their children, Margaret, George, Blanche and Roy; Mrs. Joseph Shilling and her family; Mrs. Bessie Chester and her son; Mr. and Mrs. H. E. Warbel and their family; Miss Grace Warbel; Mrs. John F. Gray of Chewsville; Mrs. W. E. Huntzbery and G. W. Gray of Hagerstown; Mr. and Mrs. George E. Gray of Lehighton, Pa., and their children; Mr. and Mrs. Daniel Faulders and Mrs. Ann R. Stouffer of Mapleville; Mr. and Mrs. John Huyett of State Line; and Mr. and Mrs. Calvin Warrenfeltz of Beaver Creek.

(Submitted by Connie Leisinger of Chewsville, daughter of Maude Warbel Weaver, the girl seated second from the left in the front row of the photo)

# A growing family

The W. D. Byron farm in Williamsport stood where the town's water works is located today. William and Nora Fearnow lived and worked there, raising a family of nine boys and one girl. Some of the family are pictured in this 1914 photo, while others were yet to come. From left: an unidentified farm hand, William, Nora, Lloyd, Orville, Norman, Lola, unidentified and George. Sitting on a basin on the back porch is James.

(Submitted by Frank Fearnow of Hagerstown, who was one of those yet to come)

# Men on the moon

Charles Hawn, center, and his buddies worked in passenger service for the Pennsylvania Railroad. When they got a day off to attend the Hagerstown Fair in September 1913, they lit up some stogies and reached for the stars, or at least for the moon. Hawn wrote on the back of this photo, "So you see, I was the first man to sit on the moon."

Two of the men pictured with Hawn are J.W. Brown and L. C. Purdham. The other two are unidentified.

The photo was submitted by Jane Hixson of Hagerstown, the daughter of Charles Hawn. She remembers going to the "Great Hagerstown Fair" later on, in the 1920s, before she was 10 years old. Schools would be closed on Friday during the fair, she says, so that all of the children (and teachers) could attend.

She says her father, who grew up on a farm, didn't like to wear collars, which he had to do when he worked in passenger service. To get around that, he went into freight service instead. In the train's caboose, he used to cook a hearty dish he called German stew, which he made with ground beef, noodles, tomatoes and potatoes. He'd bring the leftovers home to share with his family.

# Mail's coming

Smithsburg's rural mail carriers delivered letters by horse and wagon in 1914, when this photo was taken. They're standing beside a building on the southeast corner of the town square, the Peoples Bank Building, which still stands. The post office was in the basement of the building. From left, the carriers are: Mr. Welty (it could be John or Sam, as both were carriers), Samuel D. Newman, Frank Shank, Mr. Gardner and Max Newman.

(Submitted by the Smithsburg Historical Society)

# The 1920s

## Phone float

Taking part in a Chesapeake & Potomac Telephone Company float in 1929, celebrating the company's 50th anniversary, are, from left: Hilda Carter, Fern Rase and Laura Mullen. The other women are unidentified.

## Boonsboro, 1922

The Boonsboro High School Class of 1922 (in photo at right) included, front row from left: Kathleen Gantz, Lois Wilson, Hugh A. Ford, Naomi Biser, Lester Doyle and Harold Blickenstaff. Standing, from left, are: Atlee Shifler, Frances Alexander, Merle Funk, Thelma Keadle, Paul Snyder, Delilah Keadle and Bailey Nelson.

**(Submitted by Ed Itnyre of Rohrersville)**

## At a crossroads

Like many public school teachers at the time, Victorine Mumma of Sharpsburg got a certificate to teach right out of high school. She would have been 17 or 18 when this photo was taken around 1921. It shows students at the Lappans School at Lappans Crossroads, where Miss Mumma began teaching. She's the tallest one, third from the right in the back row. Later, she married Leon Morgan of Boonsboro and got her M.A. degree in education. She taught at the Antietam Street School and then, for most of her career, taught art at Bester School in Hagerstown. Mrs. Morgan retired in 1968 and died in 1971. The schoolhouse, which apparently needed iron mesh to protect its windows even back then, became a private home.

(Submitted by B.J. Morgan of Keedysville, son of Victorine and Leon Morgan)

## Cradle Class

Mothers of the Cradle Class of St. Matthew's Evangelical United Brethren Church show off their children outside the church at the corner of Franklin and High streets in Hagerstown in 1920. The Cradle Class consisted of church mothers who recently had children. The church, still on that site, is now called St. Matthew's United Methodist Church.

The photo was submitted by Freda Stone of Hagerstown, whose husband, Robert F. Stone, can be seen in the arms of his mother, Susan Alice Stone, just below the right side of the window on the left.

## Frog Hollow business

There's an area near where Antietam Creek runs into the Potomac River that's called Frog Hollow. The spot gained notoriety during the Prohibition years (1920-1933) as a favorite area for moonshiners. In this photo taken around 1920, federal Internal Revenue agents known as "revenuers" had just discovered an illegal still and had their photo taken with it before destroying it.
(Submitted by Doug Bast of Boonsboro)

## Toll house

The Old Bank Road toll house stood on the National Pike west of Hancock, on what is now Md. 144. Photographed around 1920, the toll house is the taller building on the left. The building next to it was used for storage. The gentleman beside it is unidentified. The toll house, built in 1863, has been completely restored. In its heyday, it charged six cents for the passage of every score of sheep or hogs, 12 cents per score of cattle, four cents for each horse and rider, and three cents for every led or driven horse, mule or ass. You'd also shell out 12 cents for "every chariot, coach, cochee, stage, phaeton, chaise with two horse and four wheels."
(Submitted by the Hancock Historical Society)

## Bound for glory

Some smartly dressed men sit beside the railroad station in Smithsburg, probably in the early 1920s. They appear to be waiting to catch a train, perhaps for a day excursion to Pen Mar Park. The station still stands on Railroad Lane in Smithsburg; the track lies off to the right. Several passenger trains came through town every day in the 1920s. The gentleman sitting at the far right is Hoy D. Newman; to his right is his father, Samuel David Newman; and to his right is a cousin, Richard Newman. The two young men standing behind them are Hoy's son David Newman, left, and at right, another son of Samuel, Max Newman.

(Photo submitted by the Smithsburg Historical Society; identities provided by Sarah Smith of Hagerstown, granddaughter of Hoy D. Newman)

## Priming the pump

An unidentified man reveals the workings of an early gasoline pump on the northwest corner of Public Square in Hagerstown around 1920.

(Submitted by the Hagerstown Roundhouse Museum)

## Winter Street girls

**Girls who went to Winter Street School in Hagerstown during the 1921-22 school year were all smiles – or mostly smiles – for this photo. (Submitted by John W. Snyder of Hagerstown)**

# Corn planting time

Four teams of horses plow the fields for planting corn near Clear Spring in this early 1920s photo. At far right is Leo A. Cohill, who bought the old Stafford Hall farm in April 1920. The boy next to him is his son, Gale B. Cohill. The woman in the hat at far left is Leo's wife, Anna Marie Cohill, known to everyone as "Nannie." The others, hired workers, are unidentified. The farm is still in the family, owned by another son, Leo W. Cohill.

(Submitted by Leo W. Cohill of Clear Spring)

## At your service

**Thomas McCullough waits for customers to come to his store in Hancock around 1920. (Submitted by Dave White of Hagerstown)**

## Pipe break

A work crew takes a lunch break from laying pipe in Hagerstown, probably in the early 1920s. The man in the front row, second from left, is Allie Repp. Behind his right shoulder is Walter Steele. Third from the left in the front row is Harry King; behind his left shoulder is Ernest Shirley. The second man from the right, behind some pipe, is George Repp, son of Allie. The men may have been working for a contractor named Harry Angle.

(Submitted by Lucille Harman of Hagerstown, grand-daughter of Allie Repp)

## Let there be light

W. Robert "Bob" Higman, the only one of the three men in the back row not wearing a tie, was the contractor who wired the inside electrical components at the Hagerstown Municipal Electric Light Plant during its construction in the mid-1920s. Higman trained as an electrician through a correspondence course offered by Edison Electric in New York. He started his own electrical business and wired houses along the trolley line between Hagerstown and Frederick as power lines were being put up for the trolley. He died in 1936.

Two of Higman's sons were part of this crew. Daniel R. "Jack" Higman is at far left and Harold M. Higman is in a light shirt at far right. The others are unidentified. Harold Higman went into the construction business.

(Submitted by Robert Higman of Keedysville, son of Harold M. Higman and grandson of W. Robert "Bob" Higman)

61

## Want a ride?

McKinley "Mac" Morton goes for a spin in the 1920s in his Ford Model T roadster, which he called his "Hupmobile." A native of McConnellsburg, Pa., Morton graduated from Penn State University and then taught high school in Clear Spring and Boonsboro. Leaving teaching, he and partner Frank Thomas went into the fertilizer and chemical business, starting the Central Chemical plant in Hagerstown.

(Submitted by Susan Lohman of Hagerstown, daughter of McKinley "Mac" Morton)

## Hancock Garage

The Hancock Garage was at 130-132 W. Main St. in Hancock when this photo was taken on Sept. 14, 1921. The gentleman on the left is unidentified, but the others, from left, are: Pug Rider, Frank Young, Frank Remsburg, Alice Remsburg and Delbert Unger. The garage is no longer there.

(Submitted by the Hancock Historical Society)

## Toll takers

James and Elizabeth "Betty" Bragunier ran a toll gate on Old National Pike in Hagerstown. Travelers would pay a fee to pass through the gate. This photo was taken at the Sword farm in Blairs Valley north of Clear Spring.

(Submitted by Catherine Bragunier Lynn of Hagerstown, granddaughter of James and Elizabeth "Betty" Bragunier)

## Clear Spring Cloppers

Finley Clopper stands at right with a mixed assortment of relatives on the steps of his home on the south side of Main Street in Clear Spring, the third house up from Martin Street. Standing in the center at back is his wife, Lydia Virginia Hornbaker Clopper. To her left is a cousin, Catherine Smallwood. To her right is her sister-in-law, Clara Clopper; they married brothers. Seated are many young Cloppers: in back, from left, are: Richard, Paul, Allen and unidentified. In front, from left, are Bessie, Charlotte and Pearre. The photo, taken around 1920, was submitted by Allen Clopper of Hagerstown.

# Good catch

A night of fishing with trotlines on the Potomac River in 1925 yielded a bountiful harvest for five young men, who are displaying their catch in a backyard on Wilson Boulevard in Hagerstown. From left: Russell Parker Batt, John Reynolds of Funkstown, Albert Parks, Mr. Rector and Charles Parks.

(Submitted by Charles Batt of Hagerstown, son of Russell Parker Batt)

## Extra! Extra!

That was the sound announcing breaking news delivered by carriers for The Globe newspaper in Hagerstown many years ago. The newspaper, first called The Evening Globe, began publication as a daily in 1879 and continued until 1930.

Globe carriers in this 1924 photo are, from left: BACK ROW: unidentified, unidentified, Wilbur E. Stotler, Leroy Metz, Harold C. Trovinger and unidentified.

MIDDLE ROW: unidentified, unidentified, Charles R. Wilson, unidentified, and unidentified.

FRONT ROW: unidentified, Floyd E. Munson Sr. and unidentified.

(Submitted by Gwen Berger of Williamsport, daughter of Charles R. Wilson)

### Did you know...

**Daily Mail bought by Morning Herald-Mail Company**

On Feb. 7, 1920, an announcement which occupied most of the front page of the Daily Mail newspaper resulted from the fact that the Daily Mail had been sold. Ironically, it was purchased by its less widely read competitor, the Morning Herald. The notice to the public stated: "Beginning with today's issue, the result which should long ago have been accomplished is realized, the consolidation of the two leading newspapers of Hagerstown into one organization.

"This arrangement is in the interest of economy and efficiency; it is a step further in the desire to give to Hagerstown and Washington County a newspaper service worthy of the community."

## Strings attached

Guitars and a bass fiddle comprised part of the Gibson Mandolin Club of Hagerstown in 1923. O.C. Beachley was leader and director of the ensemble.

(Photo submitted by Patrick Fazenbaker of Hagerstown, who picked it up at a yard sale)

Gibson Mandolin Club, Hagerstown, Md.
O.C. Beachley, Leader & Director.
6-9-23.

# Sense of Security

This photo, taken in 1924, shows the Safety Committee at Security Cement and Lime Company, east of Hagerstown. The last name of each man was scratched into the photo. Some of the names show up clearly, others not at all, some are apparently nicknames and, in at least one case, a name is misspelled. But here's what we've come up with:

The man standing at the far left is John Lebenspeck. The man standing at the far right is Charles Miller. Seated, from left, are:

BACK ROW: Otha Brandenburg, Ed Guth, Mr. Porter (the superintendent), George Badrich, Mr. Hartman and Lewis Staley.

THIRD ROW: Walter Staats, Jonah Itnyre, Lester Trovinger, Mr. Zimmerman, Nicola Dattilio and Mr. Ridgely

SECOND ROW: Mr. Moretti, Mr. DeMatties, Mr. Currier, Gibson Trenary and Mr. Sargy

FRONT ROW: Mr. Jones, Mr. Hetzell, Ed Tayler, Johnny Gruber and Walter Kopp

Pete Badrich of San Antonio, Texas, George Badrich's son, remembers that many of the workers at Security were Italians who lived on Vista Street and some of them made wine in their homes.

The business began in 1903 as a limestone quarry. It started producing cement in 1908 with one kiln. After a merger a year later, it became Security Cement and Lime and operated under that and several different names until 1998, when it got the name St. Lawrence Cement.

(Photo submitted by St. Lawrence Cement of Washington County. Thanks to several readers for calling in with identifications, including Gilbert Plume of Hagerstown, who worked at the plant from 1936 to 1979)

## Working for peanuts

Maurice Snyder Sr. waits for customers outside Orville Fearnow's fruit market at the corner of Conococheague and Salisbury streets in Williamsport around 1925. Snyder lived across the street from the store and liked to walk over to help customers with their shopping. He was also known to eat a peanut or two from the peanut tub which often sat outside on the sidewalk.

(Submitted by Frank Fearnow of Hagerstown, Orville's brother)

## Home on the canal

The Emmert Martin family spent the warm weather months living on a boat that plied the C&O Canal, carrying coal from Cumberland to Georgetown. In the winter, they'd move into their house in Williamsport. In this 1923 photo taken on the boat, Emmert Martin Sr. stands at left; his daughter Addie is at center; and Emmert Jr. is at right.

(Submitted by David and Jo Anne Rider of Hagerstown. David Rider is the grandson of Emmert Martin Sr.)

## Ole Miss

Miss America 1924, Ruth Malcomson, takes the wheel of a Dagmar 6-70 Victoria Speedster that was presented to her before a parade in Hagerstown that year. Behind her in the back seat is M.P. Moller of the Moller Organ Company on North Prospect Street. The others in the photo are unidentified.

At that time, Miss America winners could compete repeatedly. But Miss Malcomson decided not to defend her title, believing that professionals were entering the competition as a Hollywood film was to be shot about the 1925 pageant. Her decision drew controversy in the press and began speculation that the pageant wasn't legitimate. The pageant committee quickly instituted a new rule that no Miss America could return to competition. Miss Malcomson, who hailed from Philadelphia, died in 1988.

(Submitted by Dorothy Ditto Smeins of Dayton, Md.)

## Well bread

Edgar Varner, a deliveryman for the Manbeck Bread Company in Hagerstown, stands next to his truck in 1928 with his 2-year-old daughter, Louise.

(Submitted by Ethel King of Hagerstown, another daughter of Edgar Varner)

## Wedding bells

Margaret E. Itnyre and Merle R. Funk (in photo below) wed on Aug. 11, 1927, and afterwards posed in front of the bride's home at 34 St. Paul St. in Boonsboro. The guests on the porch are unidentified, but those in front, from left, are: Gorman Ford, usher; Maude Wallick, organist; Hugh A. Ford, usher; Alleine Ford Snyder, bridesmaid; Louise Funk Rice, bridesmaid; Clifford E. Funk, best man; Jane Schlosser, flower girl; the Rev. M.A. Ashby, pastor; Merle R. Funk, the groom; Margaret E. Itnyre Funk, the bride; Peggy Schlosser, flower girl; Atlee Shifler, usher; Geraldine Ford Moser, maid of honor; Harold Blickenstaff, usher; and Lana Chaney Long, vocalist.

Margaret E. Itnyre Funk, known as "Peg," taught elementary school in Sharpsburg and later at Winter Street, Howard Street and Salem Avenue elementary schools in Hagerstown. She also directed the youth choir at Trinity Lutheran Church in Boonsboro. Merle R. Funk taught English and became principal of Boonsboro Junior High School.

(Submitted by Ed Itnyre of Rohrersville, nephew of the bride)

## Reeder's vision

Roy C. Reeder was a farmer and dairyman in Boonsboro who served on the board of directors of Boonsboro Bank. He is best known for founding and operating Reeders Memorial Home on a 30-acre property in the town. He is shown here in the 1920s with his wife, Mae Myers Reeder of Keedysville.

(Submitted by Dennis Reeder of Clear Spring)

## The New Deal

Ed Myers, behind the counter at right, owned The New Deal Cafe in Hagerstown. It was at the corner of Salem Avenue and Foundry Street, which is now Burhans Boulevard. It was more a "stag" bar than a restaurant, as no women or children were allowed.

This photo, taken in the late 1920s or early 1930s, was submitted by Betty Smith of Hagerstown, whose father, Daniel D. Herman Barner, is shown seated at the back of the room.

## Family altar

Three members of the Halligan family were altar boys at St. Mary Catholic Church in Hagerstown in 1925. In the back row, second from left, is John. J. "Jack" Halligan. Fourth from left is Robert Kuhn. Rodney Wolf is on the far right. In the third row back, third from the left is Frances Xavier Halligan, and at far right is Thomas E. "Ned" Halligan.

(Submitted by Kathleen Reed of Hagerstown, daughter of Thomas E. "Ned" Halligan)

## Catalpa Church

Catalpa Church, shown here in the late 1920s, is at Cohill's Station in Hancock. Built in 1899, it still stands today, known as Catalpa United Methodist Church. It was named for the Catalpa Indians who roamed in the area. The church holds about 75 people and was usually filled for Sunday services. The windows were raised so people standing outside could see and hear. The people in this photo are not identified.

Cohill's Station is close to the Potomac River. It was a stopping point on the Western Maryland Railroad for loading apples. Edmund P. Cohill owned apple orchards. The largest orchards in Maryland used to be in Hancock. None is left today.

(Submitted by the Hancock Historical Society)

## Team players

The Hagerstown High School football team poses in front of Hagerstown Country Club on Northern Avenue for this 1927 photo. The building is now the American Legion. The names of four of the players in the front row, from left, are Widmyer, R. Dudley, Dorsey and Staton. One of the five is unidentified, but we don't know which one that is.

Those in the middle row, from left, are: Eddie Semler (coach, standing), W. Campbell, Barton, Kline, Hutchins, Stine, Hall, Wellinger, H. Holsinger, Nichols, Garonzik and Roof (manager, standing)

In the back row, from left, are: Stotler, Sinn, Garonzik, Shackelford, Vouch, K. Dudley, Rice, A. Campbell, Slick, Petticord, Metz, Gruber and B. Dorsey

(Submitted by Charlie Brown of Rest Haven Funeral Home in Hagerstown)

## Hoffman hoopsters

Hoffman Chevrolet, based in Hagerstown, had a branch in Hancock which sponsored a baskeball team named, appropriately, "Hoffman Chevrolet." Players and sponsors for the 1928-29 season were, from left:

BACK ROW: Lou Gerber, Albert French, Lloyd Powers, Hart McKinley, Jim Resley and Jack Caspar.

FRONT ROW: Mr. Smith (a deaf mute whom everyone called "Smitty"), Chester Hahne, Hap Powers, Ralph Buchanan and Bill McCulloh.

(Submitted by the Hancock Historical Society)

## Ridge Avenue School

Ada Smith (center, at back) was described as a "great teacher" by the person who wrote on the back of this photo. Also written was the location: Ridge Avenue School, Hagerstown, Md.; the date: 1928; and the names of three students: Rene Wetzel, June Ambrose and Roger Kershner.

(Submitted by June Hose of Hagerstown)

## Camera shy

John Carter appeared to be too engrossed in his reading to look at the camera when this photo was taken, but his wife, Amelia Turner Carter, was more obliging. The photo was taken in 1929, next to their home at 2409 Virginia Ave. in Williamsport. Amelia Carter worked at the Wharf Restaurant in Hagerstown for 14 years.

(John and Amelia Carter were the great-uncle and great-aunt of Gary Carter of Hagerstown, who submitted this photo)

## Park patrons

Alice and Walter Widmeyer donated the land for Widmeyer Memorial Park, which opened in 1929 in Hancock. (Submitted by Leroy Divel of Clear Spring)

# The 1930s

## *H*offman's Inn

Mr. and Mrs. Fred Hoffman, standing with an unidentified child, owned Hoffman's Inn on old U.S. 40 west of Hancock. The photo was taken in the late 1920s or early 1930s. The building is now a private residence.

(Submitted by the Hancock Historical Society)

## Sisters!

Edgar and Minnie Pitcock Turner were born in Washington County in the late 1880s. Around 1930, they had this picture taken of their daughters, from left, Frances, Helen and Margaret. Another daughter died at age three in the flu epidemic of 1918-19. Edgar Turner ran his own bakery in the 1930s, behind their home on South Cannon Avenue between East Antietam and East Washington streets. After World War II broke out, he went to work for Fairchild Industries at one of its many plants in Washington County, at the corner of South Cannon and East Washington streets. Of their three daughters, only Margaret stayed in Washington County, where she married D.C. Miller and worked for both Potomac Edison and Home Federal.

**(Submitted by David E. Miller of Clear Spring, son of Margaret Miller)**

## Park people

Richard "Doc" Nigh and his wife, Alethea Eckstine Nigh, enjoy a walk in the park in Washington County in 1933. The couple particularly enjoyed strolling in Hagerstown's City Park and at Fort Frederick. Doc Nigh worked for Southern Shoe, Fairchild Aircraft and Mack Trucks.

**(Submitted by Rose Barger of Hagerstown, daughter of Richard "Doc" and Alethea Nigh)**

# *T*wo-horse job

Tenant farmer Charles Martin Kendle plows a field around 1930 on Broadfording Road, west of Hagerstown, where the Sunny Spot Dairy Farm used to be.

(Contributed by George P. Socks Jr. of Boonsboro, grandson of Charles Martin Kendle)

## *Did you know...*

In 1930, the first line of retail frozen foods went on display in Springfield, Mass., with products manufactured under the Birdseye brand.

The first product line included 18 cuts of meat, spinach, peas, oysters, fish fillets and a variety of fruits. Source: Frozen Food Age, December 2002.

## The icemen cometh

**Deliverymen for the T.S. Michael Ice Plant stand in front of the building at the corner of Mulberry and McComas streets in Hagerstown in 1931. The building, which is still standing, faces onto McComas Street, next to the railroad tracks. George Ebersole, one of the deliverymen,**

is standing with his arms crossed to the left of the fold at the center of the picture. The other drivers are unidentified. Ebersole went on to have his own milk route. T.S. Michael sold the plant and bought the Hagerstown Ice Company on Lee Street.
  (Submitted by Gary Carter of Hagerstown, grandson of George Ebersole)

## Milling around

A warehouse next to railroad tracks in Keedysville was used as an office and for storage for the Keedysville Milling Company. The gentleman on the left in front of the warehouse is the company's owner and operator, W.C. Geeting. This photo, taken in the mid-1930s, was submitted by Elaine Strausner of Middletown.

## Chewsville couple

James and Fannie May Scadden Lowman lived on a small farm near Chewsville. They sold vegetables, homemade bread and potato chips at Hagerstown's City Market to help them support their family of 12 children. Their children are Leila Marker, Virgie Swope, Myrtle Sprecher, Gertie Bowman, Florence Gearhart, John Lowman, Edna Shaffer, Irene Butts, James Lowman, Margaret Crider, Marie Marconi and Clara Baker.

This photo was taken in the early 1930s in front of their home on Beck Road. The house is still standing.

(Submitted by Betty Sellers of State Line, Pa., granddaughter of Virgie Swope)

## Message waiting

Western Union messengers delivered telegrams by bicycle in 1934, when this photo was taken. They were paid one-half cent per message delivered and worked in all kinds of weather. This photo was taken in front of the Western Union office on West Washington Street, at the west side of what is now a Waypoint Bank branch.

During World War II, the messengers often had to deliver notices of soldiers' deaths.

From left: P.K. Kershner, unidentified, Shell Snowden, Charlie Heckman, Gabby Spigler and Ray Shirey.

(Photo submitted by Rayetta Schindel of Hagerstown, daughter of Ray Shirey. Names provided by Gabby Spigler of Hagerstown)

CHAMPIONS of INDUSTRIAL LEAGUE - 1930

# Shoe & Legging champs

A baseball team sponsored by the Hagerstown Shoe & Legging Company won the championship of the Industrial League in 1930. The player sitting at the far right with his ankles crossed is Glenn E. Brown. The business, at the corner of Franklin and Prospect streets, was later sold and became the Cannon Shoe Company.

(Submitted by Laurel Brown of Hagerstown, daughter of Glenn E. Brown)

# What'll it be?

Russell W. Ambrose Sr. tends bar at Morris Frock Post 42 of the American Legion at its former location at 25 W. Antietam St. in Hagerstown, which is now the site of the Owls Club. A sign behind the bar dates the photo: "You Can Pay Your 1935 Dues Here." **(Submitted by Raymond Ambrose of Hagerstown, son of the bartender)**

# Hog-tied

Veterinarian Dr. Ed Graves, at left in photo at left, repairs an intestinal rupture in a hog on the Russell Divel farm in Hancock in 1935. Helping him are Marshall Divel, center; Russell Divel, standing at right; and "Boogs" Hixon, kneeling. The hog survived.

Dr. Graves, a popular veterinarian and a prominent citizen of Hancock, was born in 1875. He was an assistant for 20 years to a veterinary surgeon in Hagerstown named Dr. Cousins. Later, he passed an exam to be certified as a vet himself, returned to Hancock and established a lucrative practice. He had a rare capacity for making and keeping friends. He was a religious man and a member of the St. Thomas Episcopal Church in Hancock for more than 50 years. He was known to pause for a moment of prayer before every operation. The photo below also shows Dr. Graves in the 1930s.

(Photo at left submitted by Leroy Divel of Clear Spring, son of Russell Divel. Photo below submitted by Leon Brumback of Hagerstown. Additional information provided by Betty and Jim Beeler of Hancock)

## 1937 champs

The Hagerstown football team of 1937 might look out of place at the Super Bowl of today, but this team won a championship anyway. The team was composed of young men who quit school and joined pickup teams. They practiced wherever they could and usually played where E. Russell Hicks Middle School stands today on South Potomac Street. They would play teams from Martinsburg, Waynesboro and even as far away as Baltimore, but they never traveled because they didn't have transportation. Team members joined the Pioneer Hook and Ladder Company because they didn't have showers at home; they could go there after practice to clean up.

The players, from left, are: BACK ROW: Gabby Spigler, Lefty Morris and Turk Shupp. MIDDLE ROW: Thadis Knode, Gump Andrews, Dick Trovinger and Elmer Hoover. FRONT ROW: Don Williams, Dick Snyder, Duck Higgs, Prep Moats and Ray Shirey.

(Submitted by Rayetta Schindel of Hagerstown, daughter of Ray Shirey, with thanks to Gabby Spigler of Hagerstown, who remembered a lot of first names from days gone by)

## And then they rested

The kitchen crew cooked and served many a meal to many a parishioner at St. John's Evangelical Lutheran Church in Hagerstown. The workers in this 1930s photo taken in the church kitchen are, from left: standing, Josephine Dysert and Clara Krotzer; seated, Mrs. Kephart, Mary Doub and Mrs. Bovey.
(Submitted by Barbara Reynolds of Hagerstown, from the archives of St. John's Evangelical Lutheran Church)

## Hay wagon

Twelve-year-old Charles Shank holds the reins of the wagon that his father, Howard Shank, will load with hay. This photo was taken in 1936 on their farm on Pennsylvania Avenue, north of Hagerstown. Once in the barn, the wheat grain would be put through a threshing machine that would blow it outside into a mountain of straw (visible at right in background), where the cattle would feed.

(Submitted by Charles Shank of Hagerstown)

# Thirsty?

Employees Dixie Heefner, Rex Gaver and Paul Shank, from left, wait for customers in a Peoples Drug Store in Hagerstown in the 1930s. The store stood on the corner of West Franklin and Jonathan streets, on the site occupied forr years by Gibney Florist. Opened in 1928 or 1929, it was one of two Peoples stores in town, the other being at 17-19 W. Washington St., which opened in 1926. Things began to change in 1958, when the Franklin Street store moved to the South End Shopping Center, the Washington Street store closed and Peoples opened on Public Square, in a new building where the Keystone Luncheonette had stood. Shank, who lives in Hagerstown, started working for Peoples in 1929. He worked in both stores, starting out at the soda counter. He moved on to the cigar counter, then to the drug counter, and eventually became manager of the new site in 1958. He retired in 1973 after 44 years with the company.

# Myers Market

The Harry S. Myers grocery and meat market stood for many years on the corner of North Potomac and West Franklin streets in Hagerstown. The clerks waiting to serve you in this 1930s photo are, from left: Charles R. Miller, Allen Myers and Tom Payne. Allen Myers was the son of owner Harry S. Myers. Another son, Jacob, also worked at the store. He ran "the china side," selling fine quality dishes and glassware.

This photo was submitted by the Washington County Historical Society. Additional information was provided by Bob Miller, son of Charles R. Miller, and by Lawrence Alsip, who worked for the store in 1938 and 1939, making deliveries on his bicycle.

## A night out

One of the best places to get a fine meal in Hagerstown in the 1930s was in the dining room of the Hotel Alexander on Public Square. This smartly dressed couple is being offered what appears to be a selection of desserts by an attentive waiter.

(Submitted by the Washington County Historical Society)

## Woman on the street

Radio personality Jack Watts interviews 25-year-old Louise Nigh of Hagerstown in 1936 on West Washington Street near Public Square.

(Submitted by Lorene Keener of Maugansville)

## YMCA band

The YMCA band was photographed on the stage of The Maryland Theatre in 1937. The band was directed by Edwin Partridge. Robert L. Ditto, age 10, is in the last row, fifth from left. He played saxophone. His brother Edward W. Ditto III, age 13, is in the second row, second from left. He played piccolo and flute.
(Submitted by Dr. Edward W. Ditto III of Hagerstown)

## Wings of Time 1937

Wilmarie "Billie" Fleigh Hopkins stands on B&O Engine #25, "William Mason," at the Hagerstown Fairgrounds while it was on display for the "Wings of Time" pageant in 1937. Temporary Western Maryland Railway tracks were placed in the fairgrounds. Restored, operational antique engines of the B&O Railroad were displayed. These were operated under their own power in different scenes of the pageant.

Wilmarie was the daughter of William C. Fleigh, a dispatcher on the Western Maryland Railway. His father, William N. Fleigh, was an engineer for the same railway, and owned and operated the miniature train ride at Pen Mar Park.

(Submitted by the late Catharine "Kitty" Hopkins of Hagerstown, daughter of Wilmarie "Billie" Fleigh Hopkins. Information provided by John H. Hopkins Jr. of Hagerstown)

### Did you know...

Feb. 18, 1930, the planet Pluto was discovered by astronomer Clyde W. Tombaugh.

In 1932, Shirley Temple began her film career.

In 1937, Sylvan Goldman of Oklahoma City invented the shopping cart.

In 1937, Kraft macaroni & cheese was introduced; nine million boxes were sold the first year at a cost of 19 cents.

In 1936, movie idol Tyrone Power, who was starring in the film "In Old Chicago," was advertised on the marquee of the Academy Theater on West Washington Street in Hagerstown (which was a two-way street at that time).

In 1939, "Gone With the Wind" premiered in Atlanta, Ga.

# Gone caving

Thirteen unidentified nurses from Washington County Hospital smile at the camera while on an outing to Crystal Grottoes near Boonsboro on May 22, 1939.
(Submitted by Dorothy Ditto Smeins of Dayton, Md.)

# Young swingers

The Johnny Sommer Orchestra, billed as "The Youngest Swing Band in The Land," played all over Hagerstown in the 1930s. This photo, submitted by Joan Shrader of Hagerstown, was taken in 1938.

# Remembering

President Franklin D. Roosevelt came to Washington County in 1937 to take part in celebrations commemorating the 75th anniversary of the Battle of Antietam. This photo was taken on the battlefield during his address, at noon on Sept. 17, the anniversary day.

Among the people behind him are elderly Union and Confederate veterans who fought at Antietam. Normally, Roosevelt was confined to a wheelchair. This is one of the few pictures of him standing, according to Henry Shields of Springfield, Va., who contributed this photo. Shields says the photo was given to his father, Paull S. Shields, in appreciation for his role as one of the organizers of the event. The chair behind the president, which was used by Roosevelt that day, also was given to Paull Shields. He kept it for more than 40 years in his office in the Wareham Building on West Washington Street, where he sold New England Mutual and Connecticut General life insurance from the 1930s to the 1970s. Paull Shields died in 1974. The chair remains in his family.

## Market time

The C.E. Brewer booth was a mainstay at Hagerstown's City Market from the early 1930s to the early 1960s. Clarence and Hazel Forsythe Brewer raised produce and flowers and made baked goods at their home on Virginia Avenue. On Saturday mornings, they took their goods to market. Their daughter Mary Louise often helped out and is shown here with Clarence around 1938. But it was Hazel who was the backbone of the business and kept on tending the booth after Clarence died.

(Submitted by Donnagean Talbert of Hagerstown, daughter of Mary Louise)

The Troy Laundry Co., Hagerstown, Md.

## Clothes cleaners

The Troy Laundry Company began operations in Hagerstown in 1888, and stayed in business here until 1960. Located at 59 E. Washington St., it was next to Foltz Manufacturing, where Elizabeth Court is today. The laundry boasted that "every article washed in this laundry is washed in pure softened water."

Employees of the company gathered for this photo in January 1938. Fifth from the right in the middle row is Maude E. Barger, who ran a pressing machine for the company for 11 years. The others are unidentified. (Submitted by Raymond Barger of Hagerstown, son of Maude E. Barger)

## Christmas saviors

A Salvation Army worker receives a donation in her kettle, on the north side of the first block of West Washington Street in Hagerstown. The photo probably dates from the late 1930s. The newest cars are from the mid-1930s, the one on the right is older. The Montgomery Ward building, at far right, is on the site of the former Hagerstown Bank and Trust Company, which closed in 1935. The building was torn down and another built in its place. Montgomery Ward was there as of 1937. Across Rochester Place from that building is Kohler's Jewelers. (Submitted by the Washington County Historical Society)

## Up elevator

Workers rebuild the Maugansville Elevator after it was damaged by a fire in 1939. (Submitted by Warren Riggs of Maugansville)

## The old ways

In the 1930s, Roger Ray Sinnisen and his wife, Elenora Grace Easterday Sinnisen, lived and worked in Beaver Creek on a farm owned by Mrs. Newcomer. Roger Sinnisen never used a tractor, only a horse and plow.

(Submitted by Carla Kann of Hagerstown, granddaughter of Roger and Elenora Sinnisen)

# The 1940s

❦

## Getting the message

Fifteen-year-old Lawrence N. Alsip Sr. worked as a messenger for Postal Telegraph in Hagerstown in 1940, when this photo was taken. There were at least three full-time messengers. They furnished their own bicycles, made 30 cents an hour, and had to wear uniforms and look presentable at all times. Besides messages, they would also deliver small packages to downtown businesses.

The Postal Telegraph office was on Summit Avenue; the entrance was at the back of what is now the Nicodemus Bank building. The office, open Monday to Saturday, was managed by Mrs. Minnick. There were two women teletype operators, one of them Mrs. Stouffer.

Alsip also delivered groceries for the Harry S. Myers market in Hagerstown. Later, he was a barber and ran Alsip's Barber Shop in State Line, Pa., from 1952 to 2000.

The photo was submitted by Alsip's daughter, Susan Alsip Lawson of Hagerstown. It was taken by Alsip's future wife, Bernice Mowen, outside her home at 50 West Side Ave.

## Mom and Pop store

Nelson Hause and his wife, Mary, ran Hause Grocery Store at 132 Wayside Ave. in Hagerstown from 1935 to 1971. They lived above it. When Nelson was in the service during World War II, from 1943 to 1945, Mary kept the store going with the help of Nelson's sister, Ethel Edelman, and other relatives and neighbors.

Nelson painted his store windows for special occasions and holidays, as shown in this photo taken at Easter in 1940. Seen here, from left, are Asher Edelman Jr., Nelson Hause, Bucky Beard and Charles Hause, Nelson's father.

(Submitted by Asher S. Edelman Jr. of Waynesboro, Pa., nephew of Nelson Hause and son of Ethel Edelman)

## Summer fashion

It hasn't moved, but it's on Dogwood Drive in Greenberry Hills now. But when this photo was taken in 1940, the J. Troup house was smack in the middle of a farm halfway between Hagerstown and Williamsport.
Four members of the Troup family put on their best summer dresses to pose out-side by the water pump next to the house. It was a hot July after-noon of that year. Standing at center is the matriarch of the family, Cora Strite Troup, surrounded by her three daughters. To her right is Mary Beth Troup McDuffee; to her left is Joanne Troup Bates. Seated in front of them is Christine Troup McAdams.

(Submitted by Barbara Hoover of Hagerstown, daughter of Christine Troup McAdams)

## Home

Home for Isaac R. and Caroline Shank Wolfinger was a dairy farm called Cool Brook Farm. It was in the community of Reid, north of Hagerstown off Lehmans Mill Road. This photo, taken around 1940, was submitted by Ed Beeler of Waynesboro, Pa., a great-nephew of Isaac and Caroline Wolfinger.

## Thanks be

Students at Lappans School take part in a Thanksgiving program inside the schoolhouse in November 1940. (Submitted by Lucille Bitner Murray of Fairplay, who is seated at the far left edge of the paper fireplace)

## Eavey's legacy

Jacob E. Eavey was born in 1850, one of nine children of Samuel and Catharine Eavey of Portersville, Pa. He moved to Keedysville in 1871 and worked in the tinware business. In 1875 he opened a grocery store on Main Street and operated it for more than 50 years. In his later years, Jacob was assisted by his son Roy. Jacob died in 1948 at age 97, and Roy kept the store going until his death in 1951.

This photo of Jacob was taken in the early 1940s. It was submitted by Dorothy Ditto Smeins of Dayton, Md., his great-granddaughter.

## The Reichard boys and friend

Brothers Robert Reichard, Charles Edwin Reichard and James Martin Reichard, from left, pose with family friend Franklin Shank on an old Ford tractor in front of the wagon shed on the Reichard farm south of Huyetts Crossroads, west of Hagerstown. This photo was taken in 1940 or 1941, before Robert Reichard joined the U.S. Army, where he participated in the D-Day landing at Normandy in June 1944. (Submitted by Judy Reichard of Falling Waters, W.Va., wife of James Martin Reichard)

# Penal plasterer

George W. Lushbaugh Sr. was a well-known Hagerstown plasterer and a driving force of the local plasterers' union. When the Maryland State Penal farm was being built in 1941, Lushbaugh was chosen to become foreman of a crew of inmates to do the plastering in the huge limestone structure. The building, designed to house 900 prisoners, replaced a temporary frame barracks built in 1931. Many of the construction materials were supplied by the Maugansville Elevator and Lumber Company, managed by Adam Martin and his partner Mark Petre. Lushbaugh, one of six children, was born in Hagerstown in 1888 and died in 1972.

Tis photo, taken in October 1941, first appeared in a trade publication. It was submitted by Margaret Richards of Hagerstown, daughter of George W. Lushbaugh Sr.

# Training for sheet metal

John Long was the trainer for the first class of women preparing for work in the sheet metal department at Fairchild Aircraft. In this photo taken on Aug. 15, 1941, he sits with his class on the steps of the old Hagerstown High School on Potomac Avenue. In the front row, the second woman from the left is Jane Gochenour. Third from the left is Mary Barkdoll Clever. In the back row, the third from the left is Lucille Barkdoll, Mary's sister-in-law.

(Submitted by Mary Barkdoll Clever of Hagerstown)

## Ridge Avenue School

Students at Ridge Avenue School try to sit still for this photo taken in 1944. The four-room school was on Brewer Avenue in Hagerstown. Kindergarten was in the basement. The first-, second- and third-grade classes were upstairs. Catherine Barrows Crabtree is in the front row, third from left.

(Submitted by Tanya Rinehart of Hagerstown, great-niece of Catherine Barrows Crabtree)

## Leon and Leona

Leon Brumback, left, and his sister Leona enjoy a fine day's outing on the C&O Canal towpath west of Hancock in 1941. Leon's and Leona's parents were Leon and Mary Younker Brumback of Hancock.

(Submitted by Leon Brumback of Hagerstown)

# Golden Ramacciottis

Dominic and Ausilia Ramacciotti celebrate their golden wedding anniversary in 1943 at their home at 143 S. Potomac St. in Hagerstown. Joining them are their two sons and five of their seven daughters. From left in the photo are: FRONT ROW: Mary Ramacciotti Garrott Poser, Dominic, Ausilia and Eda Ramacciotti Cushwa BACK ROW: Eugene South, Catherine Ramacciotti South, George Ramacciotti, Nancy Ramacciotti, David K. Cushwa, Edina Ramacciotti Rogers and Leonard Ramacciotti. Daughter Julia Ramacciotti was overseas serving as an Army nurse and daughter Louisa Ramacciotti was a nun with the Sisters of Notre Dame.

Dominic, who came from Lucca in Italy, arrived in Hagerstown in 1893. Starting with a fruit and vegetable cart, he went on to open a produce store on the northwest corner of Public Square. He was the first person to ship in bananas, which he sold wholesale from special "banana rooms." Later, he turned to real estate, and, in the early 1930s, built the Professional Arts Building, widely known as the Ramacciotti Building, just off Public Square.

(Photo and information provided by John H. "Jack" Garrott of Hagerstown, grandson of Dominic and Ausilia and son of Mary Ramacciotti Garrott Poser)

# Helping hands

As veterans returned from World War I needing medical attention, the Red Cross introduced the Volunteer Nurses' Aide Service in 1918. The volunteers were trained to relieve nurses of nonmedical tasks. Also set up at the time was the Hospital and Recreation Corps, to provide recreational services to veterans. These were known as the "Gray Ladies" from the color of their uniforms.

This photo, taken in Williamsport Town Hall in the early 1940s, shows local women who volunteered for the Red Cross to help roll bandages. From left, they are: FRONT ROW: Doris Lizer, Glennie Lowman, Minnie Wolfe, Catherine Hoffman, Mariah Curfman, Gladys Huddle, Edith Leaf, Jeanette Harsh, Jane Boyce, Margaret Coakley Gower, Louise Corby or Annabelle Ditto, Helen Curfman, Bertie Hawken and Anna Herbert. MIDDLE ROW: Lucretia Betts, Mary Tice Shank, Lula Miller, Kathleen Grove, Ruby Seymour, Josephine Zimmerman, Rose Kottler, Charlotte Reichter, Tillie Boose, unidentified, Anna Hoffman, Elizabeth Shank, Emma Castle, Cecilia Staley, Mary Fry, Nora Zimmerly and Margaret Harsh Wine. STANDING TALL IN THE BACK: Mary Breakall, Margaret Kretsinger, Mary Mish and Margaret Zeller or Irene Zimmerly.

Edith Leaf, in dark dress at the center of the front row, headed the Red Cross in Williamsport during World War II, and also was director of Leaf Funeral Home, now Osborne's Funeral Home in Williamsport.

This photo was submitted by the Williamsport Town Museum. Many thanks to readers who called in with identifications. In some cases, there were conflicts, but in general we used the names written on the back of a copy of the photo by Doris Lizer, who's at the far left in the front row. It was submitted by her daughter, Nancy Burger of Williamsport.

## Pharmacist Bob

Robert "Bob" Chatkin moved to Hagerstown from Pennsylvania in 1924. The following year, he opened Chatkin's Pharmacy at 401 Summit Ave., in the Moller Apartment building near City Park. He passed it on to his son, William "Bill" Chatkin, who kept it in operation until 1978. This photo, submitted by William "Bill" Chatkin of Hagerstown, was taken in 1942. In August of 1966, pharmacist Robert Chatkin was honored by the Parke-Davis pharmaceutical company for filling his one-millionth prescription.

## Pharmacist Cy

Cyrus Jones was a familiar face behind the counter at various pharmacies in Hagerstown for more than four decades. The Pennsylvania native came to Hagerstown after serving in the U.S. Army Air Corps in World War II. He worked in the pharmacy at Washington County Hospital before moving to Eakles Drug Store on Washington Avenue, where this photo was taken in the late 1940s. In 1966, he went to work for Chatkin's Pharmacy on Summit Avenue until 1968, when he and his wife, Joanne, bought Schindel's Pharmacy on Oak Hill Avenue. He retired from there in 1991 and died in February 2005.

(Submitted by Joanne Jones of Hagerstown, Cyrus Jones' wife)

## He delivers

Tom Carter, a deliveryman for Schindel's Pharmacy in Hagerstown, stands by the store's delivery truck in the 1940s. Carter worked at the job for more than 20 years, both before and after he went into the service in World War II. Carter, who lived on Bethel Street in Hagerstown, died in 1977.

(Photo submitted by Chris Brown, current owner of Schindel's Pharmacy)

## Cleaning up

John Ingram, foreground, and Howard Weeks clean up behind the soda fountain at Schindel's Pharmacy at 624 Oak Hill Ave. in Hagerstown in the early 1940s. Other prominent soda jerks at Schindel's at the time included Ken Spence, Phil Rohrer, Roger Firey and Jerry Oliver.

(Photo submitted by Chris Brown, current owner of Schindel's Pharmacy)

## FOP picnic

Participants at a Fraternal Order of Police annual picnic in the early 1940s at Bikle's Clubhouse at Dam No. 4 in Washington County included, from left: FRONT ROW: John Thompson, Eddie McCann, Harry Cave, Roger Geaslen, Frank Colley, George Brewer and Bud Bikle. BACK ROW: Lester Britcher, unidentified, Luther Broom, Grason Doarnberger, Jimmy Ray, Sam Basore, unidentified and Mr. Bikle, father of Bud Bikle.

Several of the men worked for The Herald-Mail newspapers, including John Thompson, pressman Harry Cave, Roger Geaslen, sports editor Frank Colley and George Brewer. Grason Doarnberger was Hagerstown chief of police from 1968 to 1972.

(Submitted by Helen Hamburg of Hagerstown)

# Breaking ground

With more and more men being drafted to fight in World War II, women were increasingly called on to fill their jobs at Fairchild Industries in Hagerstown. The last hurdle was crossed in 1944, when, from left, Fern Harnish, Constance Bond, Alverda Black and Bee Ann Clark became the first women to work in the Experimental Department. Female production workers who applied took a test and the four highest scores got the first jobs. This photo, which first appeared in the employee newsletter FID (Fairchild Industries Division), was submitted by Fern Harnish Weaver of Hagerstown, who started at Fairchild in 1942 and worked there until 1946, when returning servicemen reclaimed their former jobs. Constance Bond later married Paul Dentler of Dentler Furniture on Pennsylvania Avenue. Alverda Black's son, the Rev. Carl Black, preaches weekly for the Hagerstown Rescue Mission.

## Proud graduates

Four high-school graduates of North Street School in Hagerstown are honored at the Bethel AME Church in Hagerstown in 1944.

From left, they are: Sterling "Mouse" Davis, Thomas "Tommy" Robinson, Anna Grace "Patsy" Clinton and Frank Herbert "Herb" Williams. Two additional graduates not pictured were Jane Scott and William E. Flythe.

The words "Fidelity, Courage, Honesty and Service" comprised the inspirational class theme, with "Courage" and "Service" relating to World War II. African-American students in Hagerstown all attended "Old North Street School" until schools were integrated in the mid-1950s.

(Photo submitted by Dave White of Hagerstown. Historical information provided by Edith Becks and Thomas "Tommy" Robinson)

## Family affair

Six of the seven sons of Charles Funk Blickenstaff and Lizzie Palmer Blickenstaff worked at Fairchild Industries in Washington County during World War II. The seventh, Joseph Maynard Blickenstaff, fought in the U.S. Navy. When he returned after his discharge in 1945, he was greeted by his brothers, from left (and from youngest to oldest): Milo, Robert, Henry, Daniel, Ralph and L. Foster. Not in the photo are their sisters, Mary and Martha. Joseph worked at Fairchild before and after his military service.

(Submitted by Barry Tucker of Hagerstown, grandson of L. Foster Blickenstaff)

## Block party

The Antietam Elementary Schoolchildren's Care Center provided daytime supervision for children whose parents were working at Fairchild Industries in Washington County. In this photo taken in 1944 or 1945, only those children whose arms are crossed are identified. Martha "Marty" Bryan is the only girl in the group and the young fellow at right is Rodney Woolridge.

(Submitted by Martha Bryan McIntosh of Homosassa, Fla.)

## Dream Train

Pete and Fay, center, were familiar names and voices to listeners of WJEJ Radio in the 1940s. The Williamsport couple, Pete Stenger and Fay Myers, sang religious and popular music in local churches and on the air. They were often joined in song by their daughters Marjorie, left, and Dixie, right. Their theme song was "Dream Train." This photo was taken in 1946 at the WJEJ studio in Franklin Court on Franklin Street in Hagerstown, where they sang between 1939 and 1949. Pete worked as a radio announcer for WEPM radio in Martinsburg, W.Va., in 1950 and later to Florida. The couple moved to Wheeling, W.Va., in 1950 and later to Florida. Pete died in 1981, Fay in 2000, and Dixie in 2005. Marjorie lives in Wheeling.

(Submitted by Jack Myers of Williamsport, brother of Fay Myers)

## Quality Christmas

Quality control workers at Fairchild Industries' Plant 2 in Washington County celebrate Christmas at a party in their workplace in 1946. The woman third from left in the middle row is Esther Bryan; the others are unidentified.

(Submitted by Martha Bryan McIntosh of Homosassa, Fla., daughter of Esther Bryan)

### Did you know...

World War II brought prosperity to Washington County. Fairchild had about 10,000 persons on its local payroll in 1943. That represented more jobs than the entire county had contained in all places of employment not many decades earlier.

The year 1945 marked the end of World War II and the start of America's baby boom. Between 1945 and 1960 the population increased by 40 million, a whopping 30 percent increase.

## Sub in the Square

A captured Japanese midget submarine is exhibited in the southwest corner of Hagerstown's Public Square in 1944 or 1945. The sub, an early model with a two-man crew, is the same type of submarine that was sunk in the attack on Pearl Harbor on Dec. 7, 1941. It was hauled around the country by the U.S. Navy in an effort to sell war bonds. The Keystone Luncheonette, left, stood on the site later occupied by Peoples Drug Store and currently by government offices.
(Submitted by Bill Knode of the Hagerstown Roundhouse Museum)

# Rally 'round

A very tall Pastor J. Edward Harms, wearing a white shirt and dark suit and tie, stands out at dead center in this photo of the Sunday School classes of St. John's Evangelical Lutheran Church. This picture was taken in the courtyard of the Sunday School building in September 1945. The occasion was Rally Day, when summer was over and the church congregation came back in full force to attend church. The goal was to have 1,000 people at the event, so if organizers came up a bit short, they'd invite a few folks in from the street to make up the difference.

(Submitted by Barbara Reynolds of Hagerstown, from the archives of St. John's Evangelical Lutheran Church)

# Entertaining guests

A quartet of singers provided entertainment at a party given at the home of Philo and Helen Statton. The photo was taken in the 1940s in the Statton living room at 821 The Terrace. Helen Statton is kneeling, center, and Philo Statton is at right, sitting on the desk. Among the guests are Bruce Lightner, left, a lawyer and local Kiwanis Club official. Seated on the arm of the chair next to him is his wife, Mildred "Dewey" Lightner. Second from the right, holding a pipe, is Paull Shields, and the man seated to his right, holding a glass, is Edwin Smead. The woman seated in the chair is his wife, Grace Kriete Smead. No members of the quartet are identified. The dog is Jacque.

Philo Statton was president of Statton Furniture. Helen Statton operated Maidstone Furniture along with William Beard. The Stattons had three children: Philip, Robert and Pamela.

(Submitted by Henry Shields of Springfield, Va., son of Paull Shields. Henry Shields bought the photo at the estate sale of Bruce Lightner around 1990. Additional information supplied by Tom Statton, grandson of Philo and Helen Statton, and Jane Davis, Sam and David Turner, Gladys Short and David Murray, all of Hagerstown)

## The Y's finest

Members of the Hagerstown YMCA basketball team in 1945-46 were, from left:
STANDING: Jack "Hank" Hershey, Warren "Drake" Dofflemyer, Harry Aaron and Bob Roulette.
KNEELING: Max Kendall, Joe Suranno, Paul "Ears" McNeal and "Buzz" Downs.
(Submitted by Jack "Hank" Hershey of Hagerstown)

## Make mine Coke

Employees of the Coca-Cola bottling plant in Hagerstown were served a familiar beverage at their company Christmas party in 1946. The party was held at Fountain Head Country Club. Among the party-goers and their guests were Mr. and Mrs. "Pop" Burger, seated at the left front of the table. Across from them, from front to back, were: Fritz Hoffman, Charles Magaha, John David Magaha, Mr. and Mrs. Bubba Randall and Mr. and Mrs. Jeff Frederick.

(Submitted by Charles Magaha of Smithsburg, whose father, John David Magaha, worked at the plant from 1939 to 1952)

## Roof family

In photo at left, Emma Wade Roof, right, poses with her three daughters on the family property on Falling Waters Road below Downsville in 1947. Emma's husband, Walter Martin Roof, was a lockkeeper on the C&O Canal. The house was all that remained after the flood of 1936. Water marks on the house still show how high the floodwaters reached. Emma's daughters, from left, are: Margaret Wade Garrett, Hazel Roof Baker and Louise Roof Eschelman. Behind them is Hazel's daughter, Lois Baker Smith. The photo was taken by Hazel's husband, George Baker.

(Submitted by Michele Dyer of Clear Spring, daughter of Lois Baker Smith)

### Did you know...

During the late 1940s, much of the local television-watching was done in taverns and restaurants.

## Girls' night out

Betty Beeler of Hancock submitted this photo of her mother, Clamonce Murray Wilkerson, left, out for a night on the town in 1948 in Hagerstown with her sisters and a family friend. Joining Clamonce, from left, are: her friend, Jane Rowe, and her sisters Betty Ellen Murray Sheeder, Phoebe Edwina Murray Wilkerson and Mary Louise "Wicky" Murray Martin.

# Young patriots

A group of youngsters (in photo at left) celebrate the Fourth of July in 1946 on Heisterboro Road in Halfway. From left: Brad Wilson, Don Kreh, unidentified, Frances Bowers, Anita Brandenburg, Gwen Wilson, Bob Bowers, Joann Kreh and Joann Guyton. All of them lived on the street except Joann Guyton, who was a cousin of the Bower kids and was visiting from Baltimore, and the unidentified girl, who was from Pennsylvania and was the aunt of Anita Brandenburg. (Submitted by Gwen Berger of Williamsport)

## Did you know...

As late as 1947, radio station WJEJ's schedule on a typical day included such offerings as Buck Rogers, Superman, Tom Mix, Queen for a Day, Heart's Desire, Adventures of the Falcon, Malcolm Shayne, Fulton Lewis, and Cedric Foster.

There was also Merv Griffin's program, music by famed dance bands in live performances, and local programming such as Malcolm Hutto's organ music.

# A summer pose

Dressed up to go, from left, Robert Bingaman, Sue Bingaman Wiles, their cousin Carolyn Stouffer and Deryle Bingaman stand in front of the Bingaman home across from the Superior Dairy on Chestnut Street in Hagerstown in 1947. In the background is a Superior Dairy milk truck. (Submitted by Deryle Bingaman of Hagerstown)

# Last trolley to Williamsport

Trolley service between Williamsport and Hagerstown began in 1897. A one-way fare cost 5 cents. Motormen made 25 to 92 cents an hour. When the trolley made its last run 50 years later, the fare had increased to 16 cents. The trolley was replaced by bus service.

The trolley, which could hold 80 to 90 riders, started its run at 4:45 a.m. Trolley operator Sam Palmer remembered knowing every rider's name. The trolley traveled at about 30 miles per hour, although a motorcyclist claimed once to have clocked it going 72 mph downhill on U.S. 11, Virginia Avenue.

These photographs show the last trolley and the first bus on Aug. 4, 1947. The final trolley ride was provided for free to mark the occasion.

(The first bus photo was submitted by Patricia French of Williamsport. The last trolley photo was submitted by the Williamsport Town Museum)

# Veterans Victory Homecoming Parade

Members of the Ridge Avenue Group march east in the first block of West Washington Street in Hagerstown on Veterans Day, Nov. 11, 1946, in the Veterans Victory Homecoming Parade. Injured veterans are riding in the automobile behind the marchers.

Those marching, from left, are: Lt. Max Swartz, Sgt. Paul "Mac" May, Dutch Davis, Tom Kunkleman, Gerald Brandt, Lester Stoner, S/Sgt. Roy Lint, Carrol Wyand (face hidden), Earl May, Bob Snyder, Donald Toms, S/Sgt. Bud Minnich, Seaman Butch Haugh, Seaman Bill Bailey, Seaman Bill Jordan, Seaman Dopey Myers, Red Wynkoop and Richard "Soupy" Jordan. Riding on the right front fender of the Studebaker is Charles Kunkleman. Bernard Toms is on the left front fender. Two of the servicemen riding inside are Bud Messener and Paul Henry. The civilian at left in the doorway of the restaurant with his right arm raised is Ike Burton.

This photo was submitted by Judy Kent of Williamsport, daughter of Sgt. Paul "Mac" May. He was in the Air Force division of the Army in World War II and repaired planes in the Philippines and Guam. His brother Earl is also in the group.

# Temple title

Jews were living in Western Maryland as early as 1742, when Jonathan Hager settled here. They held worship services off and on from 1840 to 1875 in a church on South Potomac Street in Hagerstown. As they grew in number, they formed the Synagogue of the Sons of Abraham. In 1892, they bought property at 53 E. Baltimore St. for a temple. Fourteen members of the synagogue served in World War I. A new synagogue that opened in 1925 still serves the community of B'nai Abraham. Forty local Jews served in the armed forces in World War II. By 1992, there were more than 150 Jewish families in the community.

In 1947, the mortgage for the temple was paid off. This photo shows the symbolic mortgage burning inside the temple. At left is Meyer Berkson, president of the temple and a member of the board. He was co-owner, with Louis Meyers, of the Meyers and Berkson furniture store on West Franklin Street. To his left is

Mrs. M. R. Lyon, president of the ladies' auxiliary; next to her is Moses S. Grossman, owner of The Bon-Ton ladies clothing store on North Potomac Street. At right is Rabbi Abraham Schusterman from Baltimore, guest speaker at the ceremony.

(Photo submitted by Jacob Berkson of Hagerstown. Historical information from a program celebrating the 100th anniversary of the Congregation B'nai Abraham in 1992)

## Box office bargain

On a hot summer night in 1949, it would cost you $1.25 to take a date to the movies at the Colonial Theatre in downtown Hagerstown. That price would include a popcorn to share, but nothing to drink. Admission was 50 cents for adults, popcorn was 25 cents, and you could take kids 12 and younger for 20 cents apiece. After the show, you could get hamburgers at one of the competing burger joints next door. Treva Seibert is the woman behind the window in the cashier's booth at the air-conditioned Colonial, in the first block of South Potomac Street. The theater later became Faith Chapel.

(Submitted by Treva Seibert Martz of Hagerstown)

## Prior prowess

Members of the W. F. Prior Company Bowling League gather at the Tortuga Restaurant on Dual Highway in Hagerstown on April 25, 1949, for their annual victory and awards banquet. From left, they are:

FRONT ROW: Gracie Moser, Mary Funk, Janice Wolf, Janet Harrison, Merle Belle Collette, Mildred Reed, Dorothy Mullican and Roberta Cartee. SECOND ROW: Richard Mowen, Jane Hauver, Genevieve Rowland, Catherine Smith, Agnes Hoelle, Edna Snyder, Louise Koontz and Paul Lowry. BACK ROW: Ernest Koontz, Mrs. Minnick, Kate Dacly, Edwin Henneberger, Helen Mowen, Dottie Mimnall and Mary Ann Geist Wyand.

(Submitted by Betty Moats of Hagerstown, who found it in her husband's effects after his death)

## Plant 8 picnic

Fairchild employees from Plant 8 enjoy a lovely day together at a company picnic in the 1940s. They're partying just outside the plant, which was at the Hagerstown Fairgrounds. From left, they are:

FRONT ROW: Pauline Imes, unidentified, Ms. Lamalot. The rest are unidentified. SECOND ROW: Josephine Gibney Coss is sixth from the left. The rest are unidentified. STANDING AT BACK: unidentified, unidentified, Leon L. Hines, unidentified, Paul Fitz, Vernon Lewis Sr., Donald "Pinky" Eversole, Lon Ridenour, unidentified, unidentified, unidentified, unidentified, unidentified, Donald Detrow, unidentified, unidentified, Dick Henson (shaded by the tree), unidentified, unidentified.

(Submitted by A. Wells Ridenour of Boonsboro)

# Dual fundraising

The Mercedes convertible, in the center of this photo, parked at the southwest corner of Public Square belonged to Reichmarshall Hermann Goering. It was being exhibited in Hagerstown in the late 1940s to help sell war bonds. The numbers on the side of the Professional Arts Building in the background were for fundraising by a public service agency which later became the United Way.

(Submitted by Calvin M. Shank Jr. of Hagerstown)

# Fill 'er up

Jack and Gladys Charles ran the Charles Sunoco station at 1001 Dual Highway for 33 years. This photo, taken in 1948 or 1949, shows Gladys talking to Charles, who's standing behind the pump. (Submitted by Gladys Charles of Hagerstown)

## Did you know...

In the 1940s, minimum wage was 43¢ per hour.

In 1943, "Lassie Come Home" introduced Lassie to America.

In 1947, commercial television with 13 stations became available to the public. Computers were developed during the early '40s. The digital computer, named ENIAC, weighing 30 tons and standing two stories high, was completed in 1945.

Radio was the lifeline for Americans in the 1940s, providing news, music and entertainment, much like television today. Programming included soap operas, quiz shows, children's hours, mystery stories, fine drama and sports. Kate Smith and Arthur Godfrey were popular radio hosts. Like the movies, radio faded in popularity as television became prominent.

# Willing worker

Thomas Frances stands in front of his house in Hancock in the late 1940s. He worked in the summers as a laborer for several Hancock families, helping with plowing and gardening. (Submitted by Leon Brumback of Hagerstown)

# High-flying fashion

Members of the Third Group Wing Scouts, Packet Troop 20, held a fashion show in the auditorium of Franklin Court in the first block of West Franklin Street in Hagerstown in 1949. The group, named after the Fairchild C-82 Packet aircraft, was raising money to visit Kitty Hawk and Nags Head, N.C., sites of the first flights.

The fashion show was sponsored by the Hagerstown Business and Professional Women's Club. The clothes were designed by Elizabeth Dimon, a member of the club.

The scouts/models, from left, are: Henrietta Sinn

Potter, Sue Betts Metzer, Helen Clark Chaney, Diane Doub, Margie Rummell Davies, Betty Unseld Morgan, Roxanne Gabe Weller Kenyon, Sue Cushen Schlotterbeck Snyder, Gwen White Markley, Margaret Myers Goodyear, Roberta Crewshanks Koppel, Betty Lou Sinn Rinn, Betty Ryder Wolfe, Jacky Dunn Gergen, Mary Louise Harner Wellington, Pamela Bean and Jeannette Rogers Wells. (Submitted by Henrietta Sinn Potter of Williamsport)

## Sunday musicians

Musicians from the community comprised the St. John's Evangelical Lutheran Church Sunday School Orchestra. Conducted by Professor Roger C. Harp, at center with baton, the orchestra played during morning Sunday school classes.

This 1949 Raup photo was taken on the auditorium stage of the church at 141 S. Potomac St. in Hagerstown. The woman near the far left with the wide brim hat and the violin is Helen Harp. The others are unidentified.

(Photo is from the St. John's Evangelical Lutheran Church archives and was submitted by Barbara Reynolds)

## Bon-Ton bonds

Moses Grossman, owner of The Bon-Ton store in Hagerstown, joins his staff to help sell war bonds in front of the store on North Potomac Street in Hagerstown.

From left: Charlotte Stull, Jo DeWalt, Thelma Funk, Moses Grossman, Blanche Sites, Ella Mumma, Ray Ruth, Ethel Myers, Myrle Spickler and Rose Grossman.

The photo was taken in the late 1940s or early 1950s, when bonds were being sold to pay war debts. The store, which sold women's and children's clothes, stood next to where Hoffman Clothiers is now. It was not connected to the current department store at Valley Mall.

(Submitted by Myrle Spickler of Hagerstown, who worked as a sales clerk at The Bon-Ton for 10 years, starting in the 1940s)

# Promotion Sunday

First-, second- and third-grade Sunday School students and teachers at the old First Christian Church at 141 S. Potomac St. in Hagerstown assemble on Promotion Sunday, probably in 1949. From left: FRONT ROW: unidentified, unidentified, Jim Plummer, Linda Niemyer, Barbara Mentzer, unidentified, Mike Mullenix, unidentified, unidentified. SECOND ROW: unidentified, Donna Stouffer, unidentified, Donnagean Eyler Talbert, unidentified, Linda Green, unidentified, Gail Hovis Cauliflower, unidentified. THIRD ROW: unidentified, Bill Morgan, uinidentified, Ernest Beyard, unidentified, unidentified, Steve Stouffer, Curtis Mullenix, Audrey Mills, Nancy Harper, unidentified, Terry Strasser FOURTH ROW: unidentified, unidentified, Sylvia Henson, unidentified, Vicki Bonebrake, Peggy Lumm Morgan, Tobey Rudisell Anderson, unidentified, William Horst, James McCleaf BACK ROW: Shorty Rohrer, unidentified, unidentified, unidentified, Helen Gordon (Submitted by First Christian Church [Disciples of Christ] of Hagerstown)

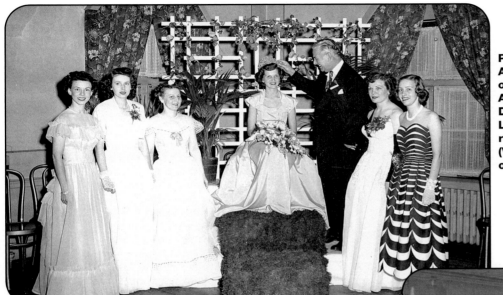

## May Queen

Arlene Messersmith is crowned Beta Sigma Phi May Queen on May 23, 1949 at the Hotel Alexander in Hagerstown. Placing the crown on her head is U.S. Congressman Glenn Beall. Attending the queen are, from left: Vivian Dean, Katherine Downin, Lorraine Leather, Lorraine Martin and Dee Ingram Wieland, representatives of Beta Sigma Phi chapters. (Virts photo submitted by Arlene Messersmith of Hagerstown)

## Dancing the night away

Participants and guests from the crowning ceremony of the Beta Sigma Phi May Queen on May 23, 1949, dance afterwards at the Hotel Alexander in Hagerstown.

(Virts photo submitted by Arlene Messersmith of Hagerstown)

# Callas family

The Callas family assembles for a rare photo together at the family home on North Avenue in Hagerstown in September 1949. George Callas, center, stands next to his seated wife, Pella. Standing behind them, from left, are: William "Bill" Callas, Marie Callas Mars, Gregory Callas, Mike Callas and his wife, Betty Kohler Callas, and Pete Callas. At Pella's side is Marie's son, George.

George Callas moved to the United States from Greece in 1911, returned home to fight in the Greek Army in the first and second Balkan wars and later came back to the U.S., reaching Hagerstown in 1921 or 1922. A candymaker, he owned Keystone Confectionery on the Square, later the site of Peoples Drug Store, then Princess Confectionery next to The Maryland Theatre. Later, he managed "The Val" on North Potomac Street, where his children worked as soda jerks, but he spent much of his working life as a coffee salesman. Mike, trained in the service as a civil engineer, became a general contractor in Washington County. Pete, an educator who also served on the Washington County Board of Education, was a delegate to the Maryland General Assembly from 1983 to 1995 and was the last president of the Selective Service Board in the county. Marie worked at the Ormond Hosiery Store next to the Baldwin House in Hagerstown before marrying and moving to Baltimore. Gregory ran the commissary at Maryland Correctional Institution in Washington County for many years. William spent most of his life in Baltimore, working for Westinghouse Electric and later owning his own business. All four Callas brothers volunteered to join the armed services in World War II. (Submitted by Pete Callas of Hagerstown)

## Mayoral race

Baltimore Mayor Thomas d'Alessandro Sr. came to Hagerstown in 1949 to challenge Hagerstown Mayor Herman Mills to a race. In this photo, Mills rides a donkey with a banner saying "Cancer Victory" around its neck. D'Alessandro, a dyed-in-the-wool Democrat, rides a bicycle with the cardboard head of an elephant on the handlebars. The policeman in a dark uniform behind the donkey's posterior is Hagerstown Police Sgt. Arthur C. "Heavy" Palmer. (Submitted by the Washington County Historical Society)

# The Marketeers

A semi-professional football team called The Marketeers played at Municipal Stadium in Hagerstown after the end of World War II until about 1951. Team members, all Hagerstown men, received their uniforms, meals and travel to play opponents in such places as York, Waynesboro and Chambersburg, Pa., and Front Royal, Va.

The team's name came from its owner, Mel Jennings, who operated a market in the West End of Hagerstown. The coach was Ed Snead.

Team members in this 1949 photo are, from left: FRONT ROW: Perry Ernde, Richard "Dick" Harbaugh, Bob Condon, Tom Young, Shelton Pike, John Elias, Doug Weaver and Ed Henson. MIDDLE ROW: Ted Schaff, "Hal" Peters, "Gump" Andrews, "Stump" Athey, "Marty" McGuffin,

Dick Berger, Tom McAllister and Ronald Whittington. TOP ROW: Don Branch, Jerry Kendle, Ivan Tagg, Richard "Nig" Kline, Charles Price, Leo Henry, Jack Bachtell, Tom Evans and "Pert" Long. Charles Price was later Washington County sheriff, Ed Henson ran Henson & Son Contractors, and Ivan Tagg operated Tagg's TV and Appliance Store on Fairground Avenue and Locust Street in Hagerstown from 1950 to 1988. John Elias is in charge of the kitchen at the Elks Club on Robinwood Drive.

There was another semi-pro football team in Hagerstown's South End about the same time as the Marketeers, called The South End A.C. In addition, after the Marketeers disbanded, there was still another team here called The Hagerstown Bears, which played for a number of years in the early 1970s. (Submitted by Bob Condon of Hagerstown, who is third from left in the front row)

# Robin Hood's merry readers

It was the summer of 1949, and school kids in Washington County weren't at their computers or even watching television. They were (dare we say it) reading books! Part of their enthusiasm was the chance to win a Robin Hood hat, in a reading game sponsored by the children's room at the old Washington County Free Library at 21 Summit Ave. Kids who read 40 or more books got a hat. Out of 795 children who entered, there were 242 winners. This photo shows some of them in their hats. Those we can identify are: FRONT ROW: At extreme left is Patricia McNamee Michael. Sixth from the left, in glasses and a gray jacket with several sets of dark buttons, is Betty Jo Barger. At the extreme right is Ecile Carbaugh Shaw. Sitting to her right is Donna Everly. SECOND ROW: At dead center,

behind the boy with his arm in a sling, is Edith Benedict Keefer. To her immediate left is Gordon Sanders. THIRD ROW: The girl in the plaid dress behind Edith Benedict Keefer is Joan Smith Munson. BACK ROW: The girl close to the center with the big checkerboard dress is Anna Jane Clopper. To her immediate left, in a dress with tiny polka dots, is Nancy Ganoe. At the extreme top right, in a dark dress, is Patsy Tewalt.

(Submitted by the Washington County Free Library)

# From the Projects

Six-year-old J. Michael Nye stands still for a second near the home where he lived with his parents and three brothers in 1949, in what he calls The Projects in Hagerstown. On the southwest corner of Memorial Boulevard and Frederick Street next to Rose Hill Cemetery, the buildings were constructed by the federal government after World War II to house military personnel returning from the war with no jobs or money. Nye, who describes it as "a pretty scrappy neighborhood," used to play with his buddies in the graveyard next door. He and his family moved away the following year. The buildings were torn down three or four years later, leaving a site which is vacant to this day.

Nigh says he learned self-reliance and independence in The Projects, qualities which stood him in good stead in later years. He also gives great credit to the local YMCA, where he has been an active member for 55 years. From his work there and his first job, sweeping floors at J.J. Newberry's, he went on to a career that included founding and selling several enterprises and writing books. He is currently president of Marketing Logistics International Inc. in Hagerstown.

(This photo, submitted by J. Michael Nye, was taken by his mother, Shirley Nye)

# The 1950s

## Ride through the park

Carol and Frank Gack take a horse-and-buggy ride through Hagerstown City Park in the early 1950s.

(Submitted by Wayne Lippy of Hagerstown, son of Carol Gack and stepson of Frank Gack)

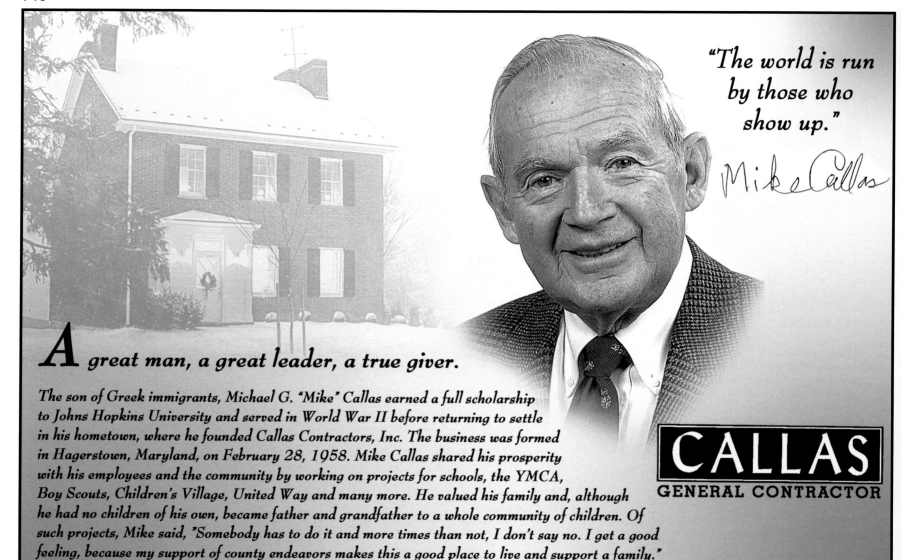

*"The world is run by those who show up."*

Mike Callas

# A great man, a great leader, a true giver.

The son of Greek immigrants, Michael G. "Mike" Callas earned a full scholarship to Johns Hopkins University and served in World War II before returning to settle in his hometown, where he founded Callas Contractors, Inc. The business was formed in Hagerstown, Maryland, on February 28, 1958. Mike Callas shared his prosperity with his employees and the community by working on projects for schools, the YMCA, Boy Scouts, Children's Village, United Way and many more. He valued his family and, although he had no children of his own, became father and grandfather to a whole community of children. Of such projects, Mike said, "Somebody has to do it and more times than not, I don't say no. I get a good feeling, because my support of county endeavors makes this a good place to live and support a family."

**CALLAS**
GENERAL CONTRACTOR

# Farewell

On June 2, 1950, Hagerstown Police Patrolman Lynwood "Woody" Newcomer responded to a call for downed electric wires in the 600 block of Virginia Avenue. When he arrived, the radio aerial on his cruiser made contact with a live wire, electrocuting him as he stepped from the vehicle. His was the first death of a patrolman in the line of duty in more than 30 years. The 35-year-old policeman had joined the police in 1947 and was considered one of the most popular men on the force. He was survived by his wife, Janet Tanaka Newcomer, and a daughter, Lynette Marvine.

In the photo, Newcomer's coffin is carried to his grave in Rest Haven Cemetery by fellow officers including Paul Wigfield, left, and Harold Lefferts, Harry Frush and Edward Kuhlman, back to front at right. The funeral director, center, is Woodford T. "Woody" Norment of the Norment Funeral Home. Two other pallbearers were Harry Young and Harley Snyder. The honor guard consisted of Patrolmen H.B. Whittington, Donald Horine, Donald Frush and Grason Doarnberger.

(Submitted by the Hagerstown Police Department. Additional information provided by Nancy Norment of Hagerstown)

# Can you pick the winner?

Five competitors for the title of Miss Hagerstown take part in the bathing suit competition in the City Park bandshell in 1950. From left: Wanda Knight Sommerfeld of Hagerstown, Diane Hetzer of Williamsport, Janette Young of Hagerstown, Vivian Walter of Highfield and Betty Gray Easterday of Hagerstown. Below, they are seen in the same order, in evening gowns. The winner would advance to the Miss Maryland Pageant.

And now, the envelope, please ... the winner is Betty Gray; first runner-up is Wanda Knight.

(Vernon Davis photo submitted by the Washington County Historical Society.)

(Photo and background information provided by Wanda Knight Sommerfeld of Hagerstown)

# Park View trio

Sidney H. Charles, left, played drums and guitar for a trio that performed at the Park View Cabin in Boonsboro, shown here in the early 1950s. With him on the sax is Ed Burke. The piano player at right is unidentified. Sid Charles was born in 1908 at a flour mill operated by his father at Charlton, Md., in the Clear Spring area. He married Winola Mullendore. The couple moved to Boonsboro and built the Park View Cabin out of chestnut logs. The Park View Trio was only one of several musical groups Sid Charles led. Another was The Society Club Orchestra. In 1985, Sid and Winola Charles sold the Park View Cabin to the mayor and town council of Boonsboro.

(Submitted by Carole Charles Leiboldt of State Line, Pa., daughter of Sidney H. and Winola Charles)

# Ready to roll

Women bowlers assemble in the lobby of the Pangborn Corporation in Hagerstown in 1951 or 1952, at the start of a bus trip for the bowling league. From left, they are: FRONT ROW: Josephine Zimmerman, Gladys Charles, Ruth Mueller, Virginia Mozingo and Lois Grumbine. SECOND ROW: Ruby Mades, Ruth Ausherman, Jeanette Bearinger, Helen Fisher and Madeline McNamee. THIRD ROW: Jeanne Price, Etta Carter, Laura Michael, Nellie Bowman, Mildred Renner and Margaret Harris. FOURTH ROW: June Price, Juanita Barr, Norma Cline, Ruth Llewellyn, Phyllis Palmer, Lorraine Oberholzer and Betty Kerfoot. FIFTH ROW: Jean Souders, Peggy Carter and Roberta Spangler. BACK ROW: Marie Dahlhamer, Ruth Dunn, Louise Rasmussen, Evelyn Heckman, Virginia Bingamin, Phyllis Barr and unidentified.

(Submitted by Gladys Charles of Hagerstown, who's in the front row. She worked for Pangborn for 10 years as an office clerk in the mailing and advertising department)

## Taking stock

Lester and Edna Harbaugh Grove opened the West End Feed & Supply store in 1950 on McPherson Street in Hagerstown, near where Byers Stop and Go stands now. It was a family affair, as daughter Virginia and son Bob helped out with the business, which remained in operation until 1970, a year after Lester's death. Shown in this 1950 photo (at right) are, from left: Virginia "Jenny" Grove Grimm, Edna Grove, Lester Grove and Bob Grove. Seated in front of Bob is his wife, Elaine Stickel Grove, holding their infant son Stanley. A view of the store from the outside shows some of the products they sold: chicks, remedies, litter, feed and poultry supplies.

(Submitted by Bob Grove of Hagerstown)

## Farmer Bard

Bard Rosenberry takes the bull by the horns on the Ralph McCauley farm on Wishard Road near Maugansville in this 1950 photo submitted by his daughter, Janet Rosenberry Purdham of Hagerstown.

## Still together

Vincent Snowden and his wife, Mayme Hudson Snowden, enjoy a spring day in City Park in the 1950s. The couple, originally from West Virginia, lived in Hagerstown for 50 years.

(Submitted by June Bishop of Fruitland Park, Fla., daughter of the Snowdens)

## Majestic ladies

Verba Almeta Buterbaugh, left, and Mabel Wade take a break from their waitressing duties at the Majestic Restaurant in Hagerstown. The women, who were the best of friends as well as colleagues, posed for this photo in 1950 or 1951. The Majestic, which was at 37 S. Potomac St., was famous for its hot dogs. It was said that people from all over Washington County would make an outing into town to go there to get one.

(This photo, taken by Linda Pitts, was submitted by Melissa Weyant of Hagerstown, granddaughter of Verba Buterbaugh)

# Waiting

The Potomac Diner was the place to eat after midnight in Hagerstown from the early 1950s to the late 1970s. Over the years, it stood in three different locations in the block of South Potomac Street north of Wilson Boulevard. Open 24 hours a day, seven days a week, it was "especially busy after midnight," according to William "Bill" Schultz of Hagerstown, who was vice president of the diner. "We'd have as much business after midnight as we did the whole rest of the day," he said. "We were the only place to eat after the bars closed. And in hunting season, we'd get the hunters coming in for an early breakfast."

Schultz hired the four waitresses pictured here in 1959, when the diner was at its second location – 920 S. Potomac St., north of where the CVS pharmacy stands now. From left they are: Carry Nelson, Jean Jarvis, Cathy O'Bryan and Pat Stalling.

(Submitted by Dave White of Hagerstown)

## Practice makes perfect

Leo Burke, left, practices football with Hagerstown High School teammate Johnny Ramer in the fall of 1950. Burke, a standout athlete in high school, went on to play professional baseball from the late 1950s through 1967 in both the minor and major leagues. He played for the Baltimore Orioles, the Chicago Cubs, the Los Angeles Angels and the St. Louis Cardinals.

(Submitted by Gwen Berger of Williamsport)

# In the know

The Hagerstown News Agency, at 45 N. Potomac St., offered periodicals, local and city newspapers, magazines, snacks, cigarettes, pipes, toothpaste and other various sundries. The News Agency performed an important service to the community, "a general store of newsprint," according to John Frye, director of the Western Maryland Room at Washington County Free Library.

Paul Troxell, appearing in both photos, ran the news agency for many years. Kate Kendall, shown in photograph at right, worked as a clerk. (Submitted by the Western Maryland Room at Washington County Free Library from the collection of Margaret Ann Wempe)

## Converted

James Brumback, left, and his friend Elwood Marks Jr. prepare to go for a breezy ride in Hancock around 1950. "Everybody in Hancock knew James," said his nephew, Leon Brumback of Hagerstown, who submitted this photo. "He served in World War II with General Patton and he was respected by everyone. He was a great fisherman and young guys would bring him deer and quail."

Auto buff Bill Knode of Hagerstown helped date the convertible to between 1949 and 1952. Two-piece windshields last appeared on GM and Ford cars in 1951 and on Chrysler cars in 1952, he said. Push-button door handles first appeared on GM cars in 1949 and on Ford cars in 1950.

## Brooks brothers

Roger, left, and Bill Brooks lived on a small farm on Round Top Road west of Hancock. They lived off the land; raised sheep, cattle and pigs; farmed by horse power; and tended a small apple orchard. Neither one married. They attended Catalpa Church, where both of them sang hymns robustly. Roger died in 1971 and Bill in 1984. Both are buried at Catalpa Church. This photo, taken in the early 1950s, was submitted by the Hancock Historical Society.

# Unhappy new year

Maryland State Trooper 1st Class Robert "R.F." Stone investigates an accident that occurred at Gower's Station near Downsville on the morning of New Year's Day in 1951. The train-car collision occurred where Md. 63 intersected with the Pennyslvania Railroad tracks. The driver of the 1936 Chysler sedan, Leonard Swain of Hagerstown, suffered cuts on his face and hand. Stone's police report said the car was demolished and he estimated its value at $50.

(Submitted by Freda Stone of Hagerstown, wife of Tfc. R.F. Stone)

# Covering Ike

Gene Corsi drove the #69 Potomac Motor Lines bus that carried the press corps when Presidential candidate Dwight D. Eisenhower came to Hagerstown while campaigning in September 1952. Eisenhower gave a speech in Public Square and then continued on to Frederick.

(Submitted by Peggy Corsi of Hagerstown, wife of Gene Corsi)

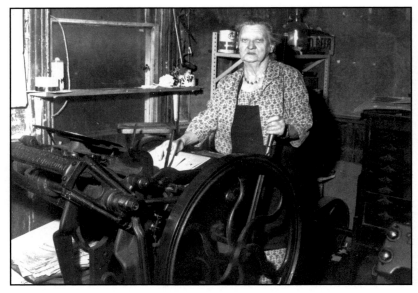

## News maker

Susan Bohler was owner of the Hancock News, a weekly newspaper published on Pennsylvania Avenue in Hancock. She bought the business in 1947 from George Huber and operated it for 19 years with the help of only one full-time and one part-time employee. Her son had no interest in running the paper and she sold it to its current owner, the Morgan Messenger, in 1966. This photo, showing her printing pages in 1951, was submitted by the Hancock Historical Society.

## Easy riders

The Blue Ridge Riding Club navigates a back road in Washington County in 1952 or 1953. The club was started in 1945 with 19 charter members from Keedysville, Gapland, Boonsboro and Shepherdstown, W.Va. Its first president was Clarence W. "Pat" Eakle, who carried mail in the Keedysville area for 36 years. Outings were usually arranged so that spouses and friends carried food in cars to meet riders for a picnic lunch.

This photo was submitted by Wayne Lippy of Hagerstown, whose mother and stepfather, Carol and Frank Gack, are at the head of this excursion.

## Party time

Dolores Marquiss Pannell, standing at far right, celebrated her 11th birthday on Feb. 22, 1951, with her sisters and friends at her home at 101 Devonshire Rd. in Hagerstown. Seated, from left are: Sarah Lawrence, Kitzie Marquiss Galbraith, Glenda Delauder, Rebecca Scuffins and Betty Marquiss Bragg. Standing, from left, are: Nancy Hoffman, Phyllis Gearhart, Mary Vera, Patsy Masser Merrill and Dolores Marquiss Pannell. Henry Marquiss, father of Dolores, Betty and Kitzie, operated Marquiss Photoengraving Company in Hagerstown for many years. (Submitted by Mary Vera of Hagerstown, who's in the back row)

# Graduation time

The 1951 graduating class at North Street School in Hagerstown consisted of, from left: TOP ROW: Gilbert Ware, Charles "Bubba" Latney, James Vernon "Sonny" Barnes, Samuel Slaughter, Henry Taylor and Gordon Dowery. FRONT ROW: Dolores Christian, Patricia Hill and Lula Hollands. In the class, but not in the photo, were Phyllis Shedd and Ruth Bennett.
(Submitted by Robert Johnson of Hagerstown)

# Arbor Day

Teacher Florence Castle Hartle (center) and students at Williamsport Primary School gather behind the school on Church Street to celebrate Arbor Day in March 1953. This photo shows part of a circle of students surrounding a tree which principal Reginald Bailey was about to plant. At far right is Joy Hartle, and next to her is Lucinda Hartle, the teacher's daughters. Two girls to the left of Mrs. Hartle, with one button on her sweater fastened, is Ruth Harsh.

Mrs. Hartle, who is 91 and still living in Williamsport, says the school served students from kindergarten through third grade. Though operated by the Board of Education, it was private, and students paid $5 a month, or $45 a year, to attend. They got half a pint of milk and graham crackers each day, except on Thursdays, when it was Triscuits and pineapple

juice. Mrs. Hartle was given $30 a year to buy supplies, mostly crayons and large pencils.

Mrs. Hartle, who taught at the school for 18 years, started her 39-year teaching career at the one-room Dry Run School on St. Paul's Road north of Clear Spring. After it closed, she taught in Downsville and Maugansville schools before going to Williamsport Primary School. She finished her career at Winter Street School. (Submitted by Robert Harsh of Williamsport, whose sister Ruth is in the photo)

156

## Future ump

Louie Kowk Lung was believed to be the first baby born here of Chinese parents when he arrived at Washington County Hospital on March 30, 1952. His mother was Yip Chun Hun and his father was Louie Foom You Lung, proprietor of the Eagle Chinese Restaurant at 27 S. Potomac St. in Hagerstown. "Ling Louie," as he is commonly known, joined the Marines after high school and went on to become a behavior resource specialist in the Washington County elementary schools. But he is best known as an umpire at baseball, softball, volleyball, basketball and football games, from Little League through the collegiate level, both locally and outside the county. The Eagle, the first Chinese restaurant in Washington County, closed in 1974 after the fire at The Maryland Theatre next door. (Submitted by Ling Louie of Hagerstown, who in the photo is wearing a typical Chinese baby bonnet)

## Blairs Valley folks

Polly Myers, front, was more interested in her Easter Bunny than in the photographer when her picture was taken with her 10 brothers and sisters in the early 1950s. The children of Andrew and Dora Myers, they lived on the family homeplace on Blairs Valley Road. The older ones would walk 3 to 4 miles to get to school in Clear Spring. From left in the back row are: Shirley, Jacob, James, Joseph and David. In front of them, from left, are Patrick, Tansey, Benjamin, Dorothy and Robert. (Submitted by Dorothy Myers Miller of Hagerstown)

## Dorbee's first

Employees of Dorbee Manfacturing on West Franklin Street in Hagerstown celebrate the company's first anniversary in 1952. The company made ladies' dresses out of New York.
(Submitted by Peggy Corsi of Hagerstown, who worked at Dorbee)

# Pangborn Ladies' Christmas

The Pangborn Corp. Girls' Christmas party was held in the ballroom of the Hotel Alexander in 1951 or 1952. Those in attendance were: FRONT ROW: Genevieve Fleming Recher, unidentified, Lucille Ruth Karn, Judy Long Hess, unidentified, Jean Hebb Smith, Myrtle Allen, unidentified, Gladys Babington Charles, Velma Weaver Filsinger, Lorraine Bond Oberholzer, Frances Highbarger Neel, Judy Kerfoot, Nellie Trumpower Bowman, Joann Ringer, Ruth Mueller (partially hidden) and Margaret Halterman. BACK ROW: Roberta Lillard Spangler, Mary Lou Kelley, Connie Main Martin (partially hidden), Madeline Spielman McNamee, Jean Suman Souders (partially hidden), Doris Miner Stouffer, Dot Laign Landis, Laura Michael, Joyce Eyler, Virginia Browning Mozingo, Doris Thomas, Gladys Lauricella, Bea Everly Eichelberger, Pat Snodderly, Lucille Pryor, Santa Claus, Fetsie Snook Cauffman (partially hidden), Bonnie Hartle Huff, Angela Guth (partially hidden), Doris Truax, Elaine Scheller, Esther McCarren, June Price, Ruth Llewellyn, Jeanne Price, Sharon Gaver, Alice Poe and Helen Fisher.

(Submitted by Gladys Babington Charles of Hagerstown)

# Call waiting

In 1952, the Smithsburg Telephone Exchange was at 11 E. Water St. in the home of Annie Schlosser (in photo at left) – an operator for many years known to all as "Miss Annie." Other operators working with her in those pre-dial days were, in picture below, from left: Evaline Hershberger, her sister Margaret Hershberger Ross, Gloria Kendall Jones, Margaret Ferguson, Marg Catherine Grove, and Anna Diehl (or Deal).

(Submitted by the Smithsburg Historical Society)

### Know more...

1951: AT&T introduced customer dialing of long distance calls, initially in Englewood, N.J. The national rollout took place over the second half of the 1950s. Until this innovation, all long distance calls required operator assistance.

# First Communion

Bill Sonnik was seven years old in May of 1953, when he celebrated his first Communion at St. Mary's Catholic School on West Franklin Street in Hagerstown. After the ceremony, Bill's father, Ronald Gibbons, took a picture of him outside the school with the parish priest, Father Robert Passarelli.

(Submitted by Bill Sonnik of Williamsport)

## Groundbreaking Catholics

The Catholics of Hagerstown broke ground for a new high school – St. Maria Goretti – on Aug. 1, 1954, on land behind Long Meadow Apartments off Northern Avenue. The school replaced one that opened on West Washington Street in 1931. Local and visting clergy were on hand for the occasion. From left, they were: Father John V. Ballard; Father Charles W. Dausch; Father Patrick E. Coyne; Father Linus E. Robinson; Rev. Ignatius Smith O.P. of Catholic University, Monsignor Francis J. Leary, pastor of St. Mary's Church; Monsignor Leary's brother, Father Joseph J. Leary; Father Robert S. Passarelli, Father Carroll Kerr; and Father Robert C. Keller

(Photo submitted by George A. Wagner of Hagerstown. Identifications provided by Mike McDonald of Hancock)

# Book fair

The children's department of the old Washington County Free Library at 21 Summit Ave. had its 30th annual book fair on Nov. 10, 1953. Young participants, like these three unidentified children, made handicrafts related to books they were reading.

(Submitted by Washington County Free Library)

## Stop and shop

Downtown Hagerstown was bustling in the 1950s, when any decent shopping trip in the first block of West Washington Street would have to include stops at J.J. Newberry's and McCrory's stores. In 1953 and 1954, when these photos were taken, three of the clerks waiting to serve you at McCrory's (below) were, from left: Anna Varner, Betty Stouffer and Betty Grams. A few minutes later and a couple of doors down, at Newberry's (right), you'd be greeted at the candy counter by, from left: Betty Hurd, Genevieve Carbaugh and Yvonne Thomas.

(Submitted by Hilda Canfield of Hagerstown, whose purchases at McCrory's that day came to a whopping 58 cents)

# Best of luck

Richard Ott, left, and Harry Parks sign yearbooks at Hagerstown High School before graduating in the spring of 1953. Ott went on to Ott's Horticulture Center in Chewsville and Parks became a school teacher.

(Submitted by Kevin Barkman of Smithsburg)

---

*Did you know...*

The slogan "Brylcreem – A little dab'll do ya" emerged in the 1950s.

Popular stars included such greats as James Dean and Elvis Presley.

In 1954, C.A. Swanson & Sons introduced the frozen TV dinner and RCA marketed the first color television sets.

The Barbie doll was introduced in 1959.

## Keystone cops, and waitresses

The Keystone Restaurant on Hagerstown's Public Square was a bustling place, according to Gloria Stottlemyer, who worked there during its heyday in 1952 and 1953. She said the busiest times were after the movies on Friday nights and after shopping trips on Saturday afternoons. "Sometimes there were so many people we couldn't handle them," she said.

These photos, taken in 1953, were taken in calmer moments. In the photo above, Gloria, Mikey DeHaven and Gloria's sister Jo Ann DeHaven, left to right, take a break from waitressing. In the photo at top right, Jo Ann pours a drink for Hagerstown Police Patrolman Johnny Brewer, and in the photo at bottom right, Gloria poses with another beat patrolman, Harold Kline.

The Keystone closed its doors in 1954 or 1955, when Peoples Drug Store moved to the site.

(Submitted by Gloria Stottlemyer Yeager of Hagerstown)

# A Taste of Italy

The names Venice and Vidoni have been virtually inseparable in the last 50 years of Washington County's history. Ettore and Maddalena Vidoni came to Hagerstown in 1931, when Ettore got a job at the cement plant in Security. But the couple had dreams of opening their own restaurant, and in 1942 they bought a house on the corner of Dual Highway and Cleveland Avenue. Seven years later, they opened the Venice Restaurant there, naming it after the famous Italian city in the region where they had lived. Two years later, in 1951, they expanded to include a motel. The complex was a mainstay and a landmark for almost 50 years, greeting visitors coming to Hagerstown from the east. The Vidonis sold the business in 1998.

The aerial photo, taken in 1951, shows the restaurant at right, with the motel behind. The Vidonis had wanted to buy the house next to it as well in 1942, but couldn't afford the $2,000 asking price. Both houses had been moved to the location from Cleveland Avenue when Dual Highway was constructed.

The photo of the Vidoni family was taken in 1955 in the kitchen of the restaurant. Family members, from left, are: Richard, Maddalena, Marta Vidoni Fenton, Ettore, Dolores Vidoni Poffenberger and Robert.

(Submitted by Dolores Vidoni Poffenberger of Hagerstown, who married Jerry Poffenberger, and with him ran the liquor operations at the complex)

## Ken and Barbie

In December 1953, a 5-year-old boy named Kenny Kline had his picture taken with Santa Claus at Eyerly's Department Store on West Washington Street in Hagerstown. A year later, a 5-year-old girl, Barbie Maugans, did the same thing. The boy and girl didn't know each other. Their parents kept the photos and they were soon forgotten by the youngsters.

Years later, Ken and Barbie met each other, fell in love and got married. While going through old family photos, they came across these, linking them to a time and place of the past. Barbara thinks it may be the same Santa in both photos, noting the similarities between the two, especially the hand. She also thinks it's rather a coincidence that both she and her husband were the youngest of three siblings at the time and none of the others was photographed with Santa, probably because the older ones were in school.

(Submitted by Barbara Maugans Kline of Williamsport)

## Elkins bound

Members of the Western Maryland Social Club prepare to take a trip to Elkins, W.Va., from Hagerstown on Sept. 19, 1953. The man partially visible at the far left is T.H. Moore. The others, standing in front of the car, from left, are: Charles C. Ditto, Forrest Q. Hoover, unidentified, unidentified, unidentified, unidentified, Pat Patterson, A. G. Bobby Fouche, Jack Hellane Sr., Emory Wolfe, Bert Delosier, Jack Hellane Jr., Elizabeth Krebs, unidentified, Margaret Martin, unidentified, unidentified, Dottie McGraw, "Dutch" Shuman, Margaret Shuman, W. Fred Mowen, Scott Pittenger, unidentified and unidentified. The people on board are unidentified.

(Submitted by A. G. Bobby Fouche of Hagerstown)

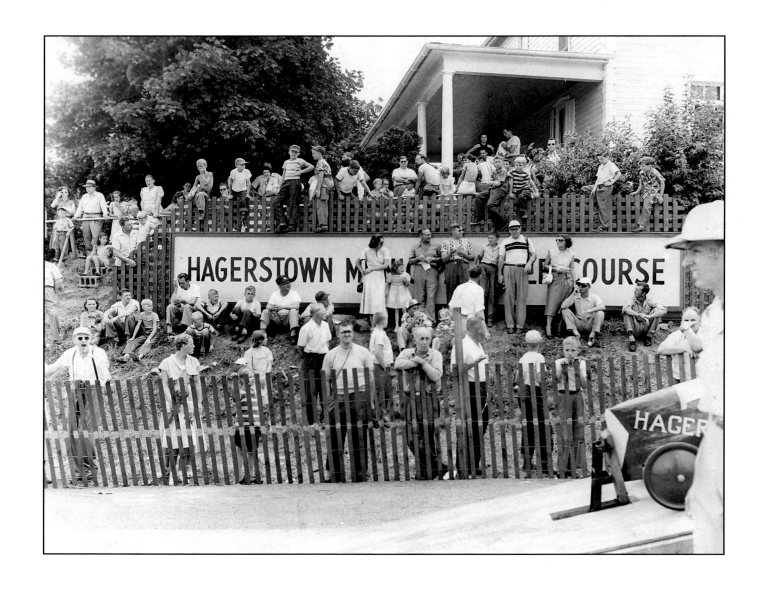

# Derby Day

The Soap Box Derby was a big summer event in Hagerstown for kids 11 to 15. Races started here in 1939 and continued until 1993, with four years out (1942 to 1945) during World War II. It was all-male until 1971, when girls were allowed to participate. Racers would build their own cars out of materials such as chicken wire and papier-mâché. The cars had no engines, and were pulled downhill by gravity. Local winners could go to the national All-American derby, which began in 1934 in Akron, Ohio. Racers competed in two classes: Class A for ages 13 to 15 and Class B for ages 11 to 12.

In the photo on the facing page, spectators gather to watch a race on July 14, 1951. They are standing on the southeast corner of Dual Highway and Cleveland Avenue, where a Burger King now stands. The house in the background was the clubhouse for Hagerstown's Municipal Golf Course, across Dual Highway.

The man at the top left in the straw hat is Harry J. Cave, who worked for The Herald-Mail for 40 years. The man sitting between the T and the O in HAGERSTOWN is Leon Rhino Flook, who worked for the Western Maryland Railway. The car visible at the lower right belonged to Aubrey Barnes, who won the first run but lost the second that year.

Over the years, races were held at various sites in Hagerstown where there was an incline, including Washington Avenue, the second block of West Washington Street and North Potomac Street from the YMCA to the Square.

In the photo at right, 15-year-old Elwood Leather holds the trophy for winning the local derby in July 1954. He's sitting in his car in the Hoffman Chevrolet showroom on Locust Street in Hagerstown. A junior at Smithsburg High School, he won on his second try. He went on to the national derby in Akron, where he placed eighth out of 153. He still has the racer.

Leather, who still lives in Smithsburg, submitted this photo. The other photo was submitted by Betty Wynkopp and Helen Hamburg of Hagerstown, the daughters of Harry Cave, who appears in the photo.

Many thanks to other readers who called in with information, including Dick Cooper, Tom Shank and Nick Carter. One caller was Angie Messner Quinn, a 1987 derby winner. Another was Mike Stine, who won in 1978. His sister, Kari Stine, won in 1988. Their cousin, Wesley Stine, won the last derby in 1993.

## Is there a doctor in the house?

There can't be many local physicians who weren't on hand when this photo was taken in 1953 in front of the main entrance to the Washington County Hospital. This entrance is now the hospital's pharmacy. Note that there's only one woman. From left they are:

TOP ROW: George Paulus, George Jennings, Roy Bell, Samuel Waddill, Charles Mowrer, Lester Shaffer, Ralph Young, Eldon Hoachlander, Elaine Donnellan, Sydney Novenstein (a visiting physician), W. Kovats, Edwin Blair, Samuel Wells, Jack Beachley, Edward W. Ditto III, Frank Lusby, Lewis Graff, Lloyd Hoffman, James Sachs, Robert Keadle and Omar Sprecher

SECOND ROW: James Dwyer, Paul Haak, I. Houghton, Walter Layman, William Layman, Robert Campbell, Earl Young, John Wilson, W.D. Campbell, William Shealy, David Boyer, Kenneth Henson, Vaughen Link, Gerald LeVan, John Moran, Dalton Welty, Robert Conrad and James Dobbie

FRONT ROW: George Kohler, Edward Ditto Jr., Richard Hauver, Frederick Dove, Hamilton Smith, Phillip Hirshman, Archie Cohen, Ernest Poole, John Hornbaker, Daniel Hohman, Stanley Macht, Richard Young, Peregrine Wroth and Ralph Stauffer

(This Simmons Studio photo was submitted by Harold Macht of Hagerstown, son of Dr. Stanley Macht. Dr. Macht was the hospital's chief of radiology from 1950 to 1978 and a founding partner of Associated Radiologists. Everyone in the photo was identified on the print by last name and first initial; many thanks to Dr. Edward Ditto III for remembering almost every first name)

## Three generations

Lelia Rouzer Smith, at left in dark coat, stands with her daughter, Carolyn Smith Owens, and her grandson, William C. Owens Jr., in the backyard of her house on Baltimore Street in Funkstown in 1954.

(Submitted by Cheryl Owens of Hagerstown, granddaughter of Lelia Rouzer Smith)

## Happy New Year

Family and friends gather for a New Year's Eve party in the 1950s at the home of William and Cora Keyes in the 400 block of Jonathan Street in Hagerstown. Party-goers include: William Keyes (in center at bottom), Victor Keyes (behind William), Madge Kent (at left), Ruth Brown (in polka-dot dress), Annie Moore, Margaret Watson, with pillbox hat, Amanda Brown, with party hat, Minnie Williams, behind woman in polka-dot dress, Rosetta Watson, Mary Keyes, Nellie Keys (who spelled her name without the second "e,") Howard Kent (with white handkerchief at left), and Cora Keyes (in black-and-white flowered dress). Among those in back are Charlie Moore (in light coat and dark tie), Frank Keyes (in white shirt), Nellie Watson and Vince Keys (on end with tie and handkerchief).

(Submitted by Carolyn Brooks of Hagerstown, daughter of Victor Keyes)

## Three at bat

Three of the reasons why Hagerstown's Morris Frock American Legion baseball team won the Maryland League District League title in 1954 were, from left: Freddie Billmeyer, Roy "Tubby" Stotler and Dick Baker. The three top hitters led the team to 12 straight wins and a shot at the state crown in College Park, where they finished second, behind Westport of Baltimore.

(Submitted by Marlene Russell of Hagerstown)

## Stu's Atlantic

Leon Stewart looks for trouble under the hood of a 1952 Buick in front of Stu's Atlantic service station at 757 Dual Highway in Hagerstown, where the House of Kobe stands today. Stewart operated the service station there from 1953 to 1957. When this photo was taken in 1954, a gallon of regular gasoline cost 23.9 cents; high-test went for a whopping 27.9 cents. Even then, some folks had trouble paying the bill; one customer offered Stewart a spare tire in lieu of cash.

(Submitted by Leon Stewart of Falling Waters, W.Va.)

# Quick relief

Waiting to sell products ranging from antacids to wristwatches to mirrors, prescription drugs and toothbrushes, employees of Peoples Drug Store at 17-19 W. Washington St. are, from left: pharmacist Fred Fahrney, Gale Koogle, Ronnie Myers and Paul Shank. This photo was taken in the mid-1950s, not long before the store moved to a larger building on Public Square.

(Photo submitted by Paul Shank of Hagerstown)

*Did you know...*

Jonas Salk introduced the first polio vaccine on April 12, 1955.

# TV teaching

Paul Wayne Miner, 11, and his rabbit, Bugsy, join sixth-grade science teacher Mildred Vance in front of the cameras in 1955, when closed-circuit educational television came to Washington County.

Funded by a grant from the Ford Foundation, the project was the first of its kind in the nation, an educational experiment which continued here for more than 30 years.

Mrs. Vance was one of 12 teachers on the original faculty. Her husband, Joseph, was financial supervisor for the schools, and her son, Skip, was on the football team at North Hagerstown High School, and later was quarterback.

All the television faculty members were volunteers, pulled from various schools at the invitation of Superintendent William Brish. One of them was Allan Powell, who taught 11th-grade history there for three years until he left the school system in 1959 to teach at Hagerstown Junior College.

Powell remembers that the "studio" was "rather primitive." It was set up in an old warehouse behind Brish's office at the school board headquarters on Commonwealth Avenue in Hagerstown, divided into separate cubicles for different lessons. Power came from a portable van parked outside. There were cables running from the van through the windows into the studio.

Each lesson took a lot of planning and preparation, Powell said, more than any one teacher could do in a day. Teachers put in a lot of their own time in preparation, beginning in the summer before the project went into the schools.

The teachers were instructed not to do a lot of lecturing "on face" to the camera. Instead, they were instructed to keep moving, back and forth, and, above all, to include a wide array of visuals in the lessons. They had the benefit of two cameras, so one could be prepared for a visual aid while the teacher was talking in front of the other.

The project had its share of both successes and failures, Powell said. He went to see one of the classes at Smithsburg High School, where it was shown to a very large class in a very large room next to the kitchen, with the banging of pots and pans next door competing with the teachers for the students' attention.

Essentially, it was totally dependent on the attitudes of the receiving teachers in the schools, Powell said. Some were very resistant, others very cooperative.

Another instructor in the TV project, math teacher Downs Hewitt, said the program "helped unify" the county. It also helped both teachers and students deal with the innovative "new math" that was coming into the schools at the time.

The success of the project led to similar efforts in other school systems in this country and abroad. Ed Kercheval, one of the original instructors in Washington County, took the project to Africa in 1963 at the invitation of the government of Nigeria. After seeing how successful the project could be there, in a very different setting, Kercheval said, the Nigerians took it on themselves. Kercheval, who taught senior English in front of the cameras, later went on to become assistant superintendent of schools.

Since the initial funding came from the Ford Foundation, it didn't take money away from other education programs in Washington County. Still, Powell said, Superintendent Brish took a lot of heat for the innovative program.

He said Brish made many contributions to the schools here. One of his most significant accomplishments, he said, was integrating the schools after the Supreme Court ruling of 1954 *(Brown v. Topeka Board of Education)* which mandated that public schools integrate their classrooms as soon as possible.

Before that, African-American students in Washington County all went to one school, on Jonathan Street in Hagerstown. Brish approached the process wisely, in stages, Powell said, starting with elementary grades one year, middle schools the next and high schools the third year.

"It went across without a hitch, " Powell said, while other school systems were "going through hell." Brish retired as school superintendent in 1973 and died in 1999.

(Photo submitted by Bertha Haden of Hagerstown, sister of Paul Wayne Miner. Miner lives in Williamsport and is a general contractor in Washington County)

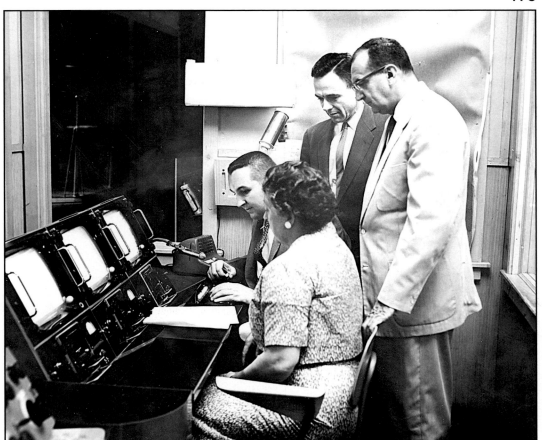

## TV monitors

Superintendent William Brish, right, watches as "behind-the-scenes" players monitor instructional programs on TV. Standing next to Brish is Bob Lesher, who served as a principal to the teaching staff. Seated are Jim Spears, in charge of production, and Catherine Beachley, guidance supervisor.

(Submitted by Downs Hewitt of Hagerstown)

# To the rescue

Community Rescue Service started its service of saving lives in Washington County in September 1955. Its first ambulance was donated by Charles Rouzer of Rouzer Funeral Home. In this photo, CRS Chief Carl Myers, right, stands next to the Heney Packard ambulance with Mr. Middlekauff of Middlekauff Motors on North Potomac Street in Hagerstown.

(Submitted by Austin Rinker Jr. of Funkstown)

# Out of business

Hagerstown's Public Square has gone through many a transformation over the past half century. As one example, none of the stores visible in this photo still exists. The photo was taken in the mid-1950s – on a warm summer day, from the looks of things. In a very few years, the Keystone Restaurant building would be torn down to make way for the new Peoples Drug Store. The other buildings remain, but the names have changed.

(Submitted by Ray and Pat Lushbaugh of Hagerstown, from a collection of photographs taken by former Herald-Mail columnist Harry Warner)

## North Street Badgers

The 1955-56 school year was the last one at North Street School in Hagerstown. The following year, the all-black school closed and students went to North Hagerstown or South Hagerstown high schools. Robert Johnson, left, who was coach at the school from 1950 to 1956, guided the team in its final year. The players, from left, were: TOP ROW: Marshall Branch, Harry Johnson, James Lane, William King and Maurice Evans. FRONT ROW: John Burnett, Howell Cook, Frank Russ, James Baltimore and Edward "Mutt" Monroe.

The photo was submitted by Coach Johnson, who went on to North Hagerstown High School, where he taught physical education and coached football and basketball for 18 years. From there he became vice principal at E. Russell Hicks Middle School, retiring in 1983.

## Generation gap

Margaret Frances, left, stands with her grand-daughter, Dorothy Jean Graves Dunnings, and her mother, Elizabeth Brumback, on Fairview Drive in Hancock in the late 1950s. Elizabeth Brumback was close to 100 when this picture was taken. In 1961, she died peacefully in her sleep at the age of at least 105. She stayed active up to the end, always wanting to be doing something and to be helping her family.

(Submitted by Leon Brumback of Hagerstown)

## Making space

Mary Alice Hawbaker was working in the classified department of The Herald-Mail Company in 1955. But she was quick to volunteer for a different assignment, to ride in the company's float in the Mummers Parade on Oct. 19 that year. The space race with the Russians was heating up. Two years later, on Oct. 4, 1957, the world's first artificial satellite, Sputnik I, took its spot in the heavens. It was about the size of a basketball and weighed 183 pounds.

This Vernon Davis photo was submitted by Mary Alice Hawbaker Kelley, who's completely visible on the float in her space suit. Her half-visible counterpart is unidentified.

## Pressing business

A new press was installed in the 1950s at The Herald-Mail newspaper building in its former location at 25-31 Summit Ave. in Hagerstown. Overseeing the project in this photo is general manager C. Neill Baylor, in hat and dark jacket. To his left is pressman Dick Grove. The men on either side of them are unidentified workers who were on hand to help install the press. The pressmen in the front, from left, are: Bob Mauck, Bob Davis, Harry Cave, Jake Kinsey, Bill Bailey and Shad Hunt.

(Submitted by Ray and Pat Lushbaugh of Hagerstown, from a collection of photographs taken by former Herald-Mail columnist Harry Warner)

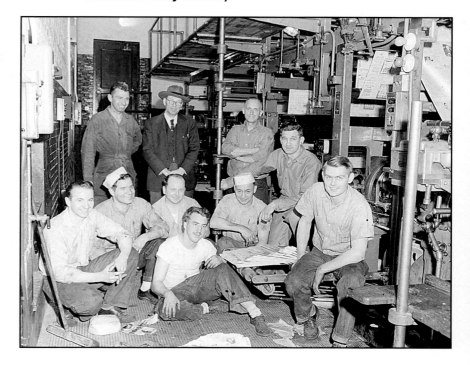

## Farm fans

Young farmers tout the importance of agriculture on a float built by the Sharpsburg Associated Young People Farm Bureau in Hagerstown's 1955 Mummers Parade. From left, Bertha Dellinger, her daughter Vickie and Lehman Toms represent a typical farm family. Two other members of the group, Joyce and Larry Artz, sit in the front row of spectators on Public Square with their baby son Doug. (Submitted by Bertha Dellinger of Hagerstown)

## Flying colors

The Fairchild Cargoettes women's basketball team won 47 straight games in 1955, 1956 and 1957, coached by Stewart Paxton. They were the Eastern States champions, the North Atlantic Industrial-Service champs, and the Maryland State champs. Joining Coach Paxton here are, back row, from left: Julia McAllister, Gloria Burger, Audrey Shade, Silvia Vidas and Dottie Martz. Kneeling in front, from left, are Amy Myers, Barbara Starliper, Kathryn Remsburg, Rhoda Helminatoller and Lorraine Warren.

(Submitted by Kathryn Remsburg Barnes of Lakewood Ranch, Fla. Additional information provided by Amy Myers McCauley of Hagerstown)

# May Day

Third-graders at Surrey School in Hagerstown dressed up in costumes for May Day Festival on May 23, 1956. Sitting in the front row, from left, are: Petrea Hewitt as a witch, Candace Carbaugh as another witch, Sharon Bragunier as a bride, William Mong as a groom, Sonja Sharer as a gypsy, unidentified, Paula Householder as a spring maid and Linda Kiem Barkdoll as a gypsy. Peeking out between the bride and groom is Linda Poffenberger.

(Submitted by Tamara Hoffman of Hagerstown, whose head can be seen behind the cat mask in the third row)

# Veep visit

Hagerstown was all abuzz on Sept. 28, 1956, when Vice President Richard Nixon came to town to campaign for the re-election of President Dwight Eisenhower. Nixon flew into Martinsburg, W.Va., that night, came by motorcade to Hagerstown and spent the night at the Hotel Alexander.

Hagerstown Police joined Secret Service agents in maintaining security in and around the hotel. Lt. Harold Kiser was in personal charge of the city squad, which included Sgt. A.C. Palmer, Det. Albert C. Lowry Sr. and Det. Richard Hannon. That was no easy job, for besides his official party, Nixon was accompanied by 30 representatives of the press.

The next morning, the vice president had breakfast with 250 state and county GOP leaders before his 10:30 address at Public Square. Traffic was cut off at 10 a.m. so the public could hear Nixon speak. In case of rain, GOP leaders had leased The Maryland Theatre for the event, but that was unnecessary.

Nixon spoke to an estimated 4,500 listeners from a platform in the same spot where presidential candidate Eisenhower had spoken four years earlier. A Hagerstown high school band played "California, Here I Come" when Nixon mounted the stand. The

Veterans of Foreign Wars provided the guard of honor.

After the speech, Nixon left on a motorcade caravan to Martinsburg. It went east on Washington Street to Mulberry Street, south to Antietam Street, west to Potomac Street, south to Wilson Boulevard, west to Virginia Avenue, then to Martinsburg.

Joining Nixon on the platform in the photo on the facing page are his wife, Pat, to his left, and GOP leaders including D. Eldred Rinehart, chairman of the Republican State Central Committee; Maryland Gov. Theodore R. McKeldin; U.S. Sen. John M. Butler and Congressman DeWitt S. Hyde, who acted as master of ceremonies. The photo at right, taken during his address, is looking west to West Washington Street.

(Photos submitted by the Washington County Historical Society)

## Photo time

In photo below, from left, sisters Donna Robison Smith and Claudia Robison Springer are joined by their cousins Barbara Feigley Smith and Linda Wingert McClain during a family get-together in June 1958. They're standing on the corner of Armstrong and Sherman avenues in Halfway.
(Submitted by Donna Smith of Fairplay)

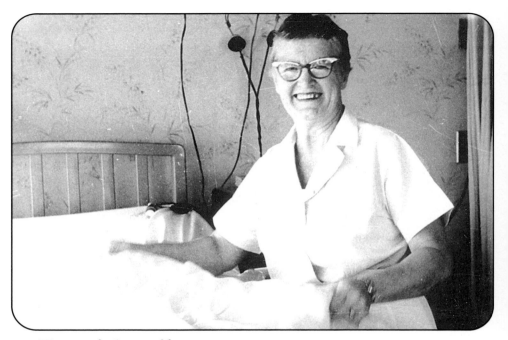

## Tommie's smile

"Nobody starts work the day after Christmas." That's what Hazel Thomas "Tommie" Jones was told when she applied for work as a nurse at the Washington County Hospital. But Tommie really wanted the job, and Dec. 26, 1956, was her first day on the job. She worked at the hospital until 1973, offering her care and her smile to many a patient. She is still living, and smiling, at age 93.

This photo, taken in the 1950s, was contributed by Tommie's daughter, Carolyn Bowman of Hagerstown. She says her mother remembers the day one of her patients snapped it, while he was sitting by the window waiting for her to finish making the bed. He was Earl Mentzer, known as "Earl the Early Bird" on the radio at the time.

## Dutchie

Ethel "Dutchie" Kimler Newman was the librarian in Smithsburg for many years. This photo of her, taken around 1950, shows her displaying some of her collection of handicrafts in her home on West Water Street, where she was born in 1895. The land she owned next door was donated after her death to become Veterans Park.
(Submitted by the Smithsburg Historical Society)

## Friends forever

Garey Martz Everhart, left, and Marlene Kretzer Barger were the best of friends when this photo was taken in 1957 at Garey's home in Dargan. Almost half a century later, they're still the best of friends.
(Submitted by Marlene Kretzer Barger of Hagerstown)

# They've been working

George W. Spielman, right, was the last conductor on the Western Maryland passenger train that ran between Hagerstown and Baltimore. He is shown in this 1957 photo with John Banzoff of Pinesburg.
(Submitted by George Spielman of Sharpsburg, grandson of George W. Spielman)

# On duty

Hagerstown Police Officer Lewis Schmidt stands ready to direct traffic in 1958 in front of the Dutch Kitchen restaurant in the first block of East Washington Street.
(Submitted by the Hagerstown Police Department)

## Big top time

The circus came to Funkstown in the summer of 1955, and Lawrence Martin, left, lost no time in attending with his daughter, Vickie, and his friend Stew Bowman. Martin says the circus set up where the Funkstown American Legion now stands. This photo was taken on the street in front of the old legion. Here, the trio poses with one of the biggest stars of the show. The elephants gave the willow trees along Antietam Creek a severe trimming as they snacked on their leaves, Martin said.

(Submitted by Lawrence Martin of Hagerstown)

## At ease

Members and guests of the Fort Ritchie Officers Club relax on the beach at the lake behind Lakeside Hall in the 1950s. Reclining at front left is Irvine Rutledge, who later served as Washington County Circuit Court judge from 1962 to 1978. The woman behind him is unidentified. The others, from left, are: Peachy Rutledge, Irvine Rutledge's wife; Marjorie Grumbacher; Jeanne Cooey; unidentified; Ed Cooey; and unidentified.

(Submitted by Jack Berkson of Hagerstown)

# Troy Laundry drivers

Drivers for the Troy Laundry Company line up for a photo with their delivery trucks behind them, shortly before the company closed its doors in 1960. The business started in Hagerstown in 1888. Third from the right in the back row is Ralph Lemen Sr., who worked for Troy Laundry for 30 years. The other drivers are unidentified.

(Submitted by Sandy Gaylor of Williamsport, daughter of Ralph Lemen Sr.)

# A promising debut

Ford Motor Company unveiled its much-ballyhooed Edsel in the fall of 1958 and brought it to Washington County with a ceremony at Fleigh Motors at 672 Oak Hill Ave., a site currently occupied by Bill's Other Yard Sale.

"The Edsel was a big thing," said Kenneth Hull, who had been a lube-and-parts man at the dealership for three years at the time. "It was 10 years in the making and it took them four-and-a-half years to get out of it. It had a lot of little bugs and it was a bit pricey," he recalled.

Bob Fleigh, owner of the dealership at the time, took over the business from his father, selling Studebaker-Packard and Mercedes-Benz autos, then the Edsel, and later Toyotas. Fleigh sold the business to Ted Younger, who passed it on to his son, Brandon, and moved it first to Baltimore Street and later to its current location on Dual Highway.

Hull, who in his earlier days had been an usher at the Academy, Colonial, Maryland and Henry's theaters and later operated a vending-machine business with his wife, Janet, stayed with the auto dealership for 44-and-a-half years, doing "a little bit of everything." The photo shows the ribbon-cutting when the Edsel was introduced here. Taking part in the ceremony, left to right, were: Mr. Poffenberger, service manager; Chester Payton, mechanic; Mr. Wolfe, sales; Gary Newcomer, sales; Warren Huff, mechanic; Dan Rohrer, parts manager; unidentified; Steve Newton, sales manager (who formerly ran a Packard dealership on North Potomac Street); Herman Bowman (barely visible), Mercedes mechanic; Bob Fleigh; two unidentified representatives from the Ford Motor Company; Jim Barger, office manager; Kenneth Hull; and Herman Bartles, who cleaned up autos. (Submitted by Kenneth and Janet Hull of Hagerstown)

## Central Chemical party

Employees and management of the Central Chemical plant celebrate the retirement of employee Leah Sowers on June 30, 1959, at the company's main office at 49 N. Jonathan St. in Hagerstown.

From left, they are: SEATED: Charles Fogg, Martha Wolford, Virginia Spielman, Frances Mills, Vice President McKinley Morton, Leah Sowers, P`resident Franklin Thomas Sr., Franklin Thomas Jr. and Frank Schwartz. STANDING: Bonnie Gilbert, Jane Weaver, Darlene Tedrick, Samuel Marshall, Patricia Burroughs, Fred Neikirk, Polly Stoops, Glen Morrison, Betty May, Elwood Miller, Ella Harshman, Thackary Brown, Lucy Travis, Catherine Maginnis, Mildred Benedict, Jane Eash and Robert Weaver. Missing at the dinner were Erval Clevenger, Richard Morton and Ray Kriner.

(Submitted by Betty Sellers of State Line, Pa., who started work at Central Chemical in 1960)

## Winning horse

Horse owner and trainer Ivan Tagg, in long coat at center, was a proud man after his thoroughbred, Chan, won a race at Hagerstown Fairgrounds on Sept. 30, 1959. Here he poses in victory with, from left: Merle Wiles, Harold Bitner, Ivan's sons Keith and Lee Tagg, Joe Bohn (holding Chan) and jockey Gail Parker. Chan raced in Washington County from 1958 to 1962.

(Submitted by Kim Tagg of Hagerstown)

## Fine dining

JoAnne Peters Cordelli, center in photo at left, waits to be served at the counter of Richardson's Snack Bar on Dual Highway in Hagerstown in 1954. Behind her is Hal Lane. Nancy Smith Trumpower is in front of her, eating a sandwich. The photo was submitted by Mary Smith Schaffnit of Hagerstown, who got out a magnifying glass to read the prices posted on the menu. Ice cream cones sold for 15 and 20 cents; milk shakes cost 25 cents; and sandwiches went for 25 cents, except for ham, which would set you back a whopping 40 cents. The photo above, showing Richardson's back in the 1940s, was submitted by Charlie Brown of Hagerstown.

# The 1960s

❦

## Ike remembers

Gen. Dwight D. Eisenhower, one year after leaving the presidency, came to Hagerstown for the rededication of the Confederate cemetery on South Potomac Street on Sept. 3, 1961. Standing next to Eisenhower is U.S. Rep. Charles McC. Mathias, who would later become a U.S. senator from Maryland. At the far left, in his white uniform, is Kenneth B. Slater, conductor of Hagerstown's Municipal Band.

(This Vernon Davis photo was submitted by Evelyn Slater of Indianapolis, wife of the late Kenneth B. Slater)

Finley Clopper firing the coal furnace of Clear Spring High School. Tending it at bedtime and early morning was necessary as well as wheeling out ashes.

## Tending the furnace

Finley Clopper of Clear Spring fires the coal furnace at the town's old 16-room high school off Broadfording Road in the 1960s. His job involved hauling coal downstairs to the basement and hauling the ashes out by wheelbarrow. Classrooms had to be warm when students arrived, so Clopper worked many very early morning shifts in cold weather.

(Submitted by Allen Clopper of Hagerstown, son of Finley Clopper)

### Did you know...

In 1963, Dr. Martin Luther King Jr. delivered his "'I Have a Dream" speech.

On Nov. 22, 1963, when he was hardly past his first thousand days in office, President John Fitzgerald Kennedy was killed by an assassin's bullets as his motorcade wound through Dallas, Texas.

## Dawn on the river

Richard Kline fishes from the front of a canoe on the Potomac River amid early morning mists in the 1960s. His companion is James Miller.

(This photo by David Harp was submitted by Richard Kline of Hagerstown)

# Eggs aplenty

John G. Corbett and his wife, Madge Newkirk Corbett, ran a poultry operation in Clear Spring for 40 years, raising turkeys and broiler chickens and producing millions of eggs.

Corbett, a 1925 graduate of Clear Spring High School, started the business in 1932 with 250 baby chicks in a brooder house behind his home on Martin Street. The couple closed the business in 1972 rather than sell it, realizing it had become too big an operation for a town of Clear Spring's size. At the time, they had more than 90,000 laying hens.

Local men hired as chicken catchers went into the chicken house at night to grab sleeping chickens. Among them were Dr. Eldon Hawbaker, Roy Funkhouser, Bud Shoemaker and Ronnie Trumpower.

The photos were taken in 1960. Madge Corbett, shown packing eggs, supervised egg grading and was secretary and treasurer of the business. John Corbett is holding baskets of eggs ready for washing.

(Submitted by Bertha Faith of Clear Spring, niece by marriage of John and Madge Corbett)

## Just ducky

Members of the Long Meadow Bowling League in Hagerstown appear to be very serious about their duck pin game as they prepare to bowl over their opponents on Feb. 4, 1960.

From right: Floyd Warrenfeltz, John May, Bob McNamee, Charlie Kopp and Mr. Barnhart.

(Contributed by Pat May Casavant of Fairplay, daughter of John May)

### Did you know...

The average household income for the 1960s was $4,743 and the minimum wage had risen to $1 per hour.

# Ashbys united

Just about the entire family turned out to celebrate the 50th anniversary of James Franklin Ashby and Elston Ida Whitacre Ashby in 1962 at Byron Memorial Park in Williamsport.

The Ashbys came to Hagerstown from Virginia in the 1920s and raised eight children here. They owned an old farmhouse at Lappans Crossroads. James Ashby worked as a building supervisor on many bridge and other projects in the area, including the penal farm on Sharpsburg Pike and the bridge at Beaver Creek. Later, he worked as a supervisor at Fairchild Industries.

In this photo, James and Elston Ashby (seated center) are flanked on both sides by their eight children; everyone else is a spouse, child, grandchild or great-grandchild.

From left, they are: SEATED ON GROUND: Shelby Smith, Luther Davis and Lee Davis. SEATED ON LAPS: Joenda Ashby, Yvonne McLaughlin, Ronnie Houser Jr., Wilma Heil and Donnie Hershberger. SEATED ON CHAIRS: Carson Ashby, Doris Byers, Emily Houser, Luther Ashby, Elston Ashby, James Ashby, Wilda Davis, Madelon Hershberger, Gladys Smith and Juanita Gigeous. FRONT ROW STANDING: Jackie Ashby, Audrey Smith, Sara Dayhoff, Louella Burkett, JoAn Martin, Mary Ann Cunningham, Wanda Houser, Mary Ashby, Bernice Thieblot, Virginia Davis, Vivian Monger, Sandy Shives, Judy Phleeger, Vincent Smith and Denny Gigeous. BACK ROW STANDING: Bob Smith, Jerry Dayhoff, Kenny Burkett, Richard Burkett, Ralph Houser, Ronnie Houser, Markwood Houser, Harold Ashby, Daniel Davis, Donald Hershberger, Don Hershberger, David Smith, Carole Daly, David Gigeous and Harold Gigeous.

Missing from the photo are Jim and Dorothy Burkett, who were on their honeymoon, and Vernon Davis, who was in the U.S. Army.

(Submitted by Carole Daly of Martinsburg, W.Va., for Gladys Ashby Smith)

# Optimistic Santa

Christmas was a special time for Optimists in Washington County. During the year, members of the Optimist Club of Hagerstown made and repaired toys. In December, they gave a Christmas party at the Market House downtown and gave out toys to local boys and girls.

Founded in 1946, the service group offered a wide array of services to the community. Among other things, they sponsored the local Boys' Club for many years. The Optimists closed their doors in 2004, after 58 years of service here.

The Santa Claus behind the beard in this 1967 photo is Optimist James Dudley, who donned the red outfit for the club every year from 1957 to 1975. The children are unidentified.

(Submitted by Charles Newcomer of Smithsburg, a longtime member of the Optimist Club)

# Mary's family

Mary Younker Brumback of Hancock, center, assembled several members of her family for this informal portrait taken in the 1960s. To her right is her daughter Lovilla. To her left are her granddaughter, Linda, and her daughter Leona. From left in the front row are: Carol and Terry Brumback, both Mary's grandchildren, and Edwin Watson, Leona's son. The young fellow standing at the back is David Younker, Mary's nephew.

(Submitted by Leon Brumback of Hagerstown, Mary's son)

# VIPs in the woods

When this tree fell, there were plenty of important people on hand to hear it. The occasion is believed to have been the groundbreaking for a state park in Washington County in the 1960s. On hand for the event, and being given a helping hand in the photo, is Maryland Gov. J. Millard Tawes, at center. The man assisting him and the woodcutter are unidentified. The complete lineup, from left, are: unidentified; unidentified; William Preston Lane Jr., Maryland's governor from 1947 to 1951; unidentified; Lem Kirk (partially hidden), a Washington County commissioner from 1958 to 1974; Gov. Tawes; Louis Goldstein (partially hidden), comptroller of the Maryland Treasury from 1959 to 1998; unidentified; Richard Grumbacher, a delegate to the Maryland General Assembly from 1961 to 1975; and George Snyder, a Maryland State senator from 1958 to 1974.

(Submitted by Marjorie Grumbacher of Hagerstown, wife of the late Richard Grumbacher)

# Bonnie lasses

After serving overseas in the U.S. Navy, Leon Fearnow returned home to Williamsport in 1963. With him came his Scottish wife, Betty McIntosh, and their two daughters, 14-month-old Sandra and 1-month-old Susan. Five years later, they had a third daughter, Sheila.

The family lived on Conococheague Street and the girls attended schools in Williamsport. Betty went to work for General Motors in Martinsburg, W.Va., and stayed there for 35 years, working as a clerk in the maintenance department. In this 1964 photo, Betty enjoys a lovely spring day at Riverbottom Park with Susan, left, and Sandra.

(Submitted by Susan Fearnow Snyder of Clear Spring)

# Grand Reunion

Clayton Burkholder, manager of the H.L. Mills grocery store on Virginia Avenue, stayed on as general manager when the store was bought by Grand Union in 1957. When the operation was named Grand Union Store of the Month in April 1965, Burkholder assembled his employees for a photo. From left, they are:

BACK ROW: Leroy Barthlow, Charlie Liedig, Charley Mills, Tom West, Burkholder, Sy Middlekauff and Jerry Lumm.

MIDDLE ROW: Howard Holsinger, Earl Redner, Jack McAllister, Robert Hull, Robert Palladino, Leonard Jamison, Wayne Bitner, Bob Ibach, and an unidentified district manager.

FRONT ROW: unidentified, E. Wolford, Joan Forsythe, Ann Purdam, unidentified, Jo Burger, Joyce Hovermale and Rita Rohrer.

The Grand Union store moved to Old Orchard Shopping Center in 1970. The original building is now a Church of God, on the southwest corner of Virginia Avenue and Massey Boulevard. (Submitted by Clayton Burkholder of Hagerstown)

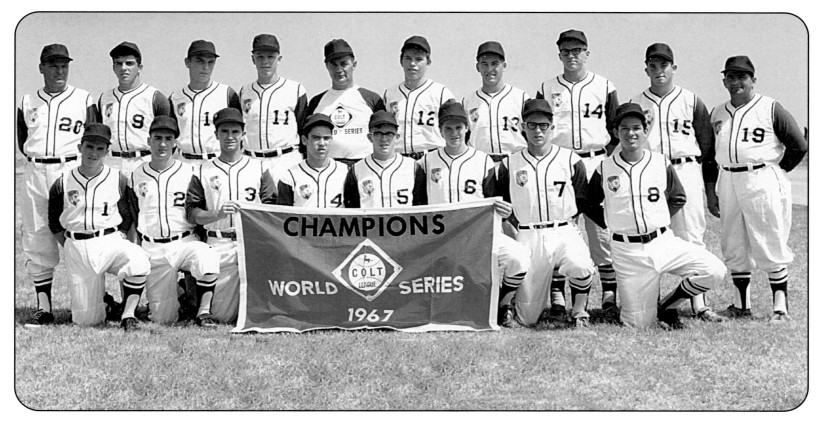

## Colt champs

The year 1967 was a big, big one for the Hagerstown Colt League All-Stars – they won the World Series of Colt League baseball. It was only the second year of Colt League baseball in Hagerstown. The team returned home on August 27, fresh from its victory in Shawnee, Okla., after a grueling four weeks on the road. They were met with a rousing welcome at Reservoir Park in Hagerstown.

BACK ROW, from left: Manager Dick Wolford, Don Beard, Tinker Burger, business manager Jack Latimer, bus driver Gil Romberger, Wayne Shank, Doug Lowry, Chris Sprenger, Buff Parks and George King. FRONT ROW, from left: Tom Hendershot, Kirk Schlotterbeck, Ed Hose, Tom Walsh, Dave Roulette, Bill Hose, Dave McElroy and Doug Holland.

(Submitted by Lois Wolford of Hagerstown, widow of the team's manager, Dick Wolford)

## June and Jim

She was known to everyone as June. He was called Jim, or "Pap." Officially, they were Dorothy June Kline and Ellis Aldridge. They ran the Dale St. Store in the West End between 1960 and 1965, when this photo was taken. See the photo on the cover of this book.

Jim worked for the Troy Laundry for many years. He died the day before Thanksgiving in 2002. June lives on South Locust Street in Hagerstown.

(Both photos submitted by June Aldridge of Hagerstown)

## Easy rider

Bobby Williamson rides a pony named Joe, one of the animals kept by June and Jim Aldridge at their Dale St. Store, which was called the Dale St. Delicatessen when they bought it. The photo was taken in 1961. No one else in the photo is identified.

# Washington County Free Library, home of our nation's first bookmobile, celebrating 100 years of service.

Washington County Free Library
Opened 1898 – Summit Avenue, Hagerstown – closed 1965
The first incorporated county-wide library in the United States.

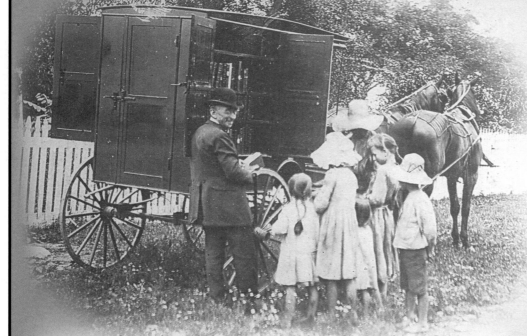

Since 1905 the Bookmobile has journeyed through Boonsboro, Clear Spring, Hancock, Keedysville, Sharpsburg, Smithsburg and Williamsport delivering great books to the citizens of Washington County.

Washington County Free Library
Opened 1965 – 100 S. Potomac St., Hagerstown
– photo by Nelson Hause –

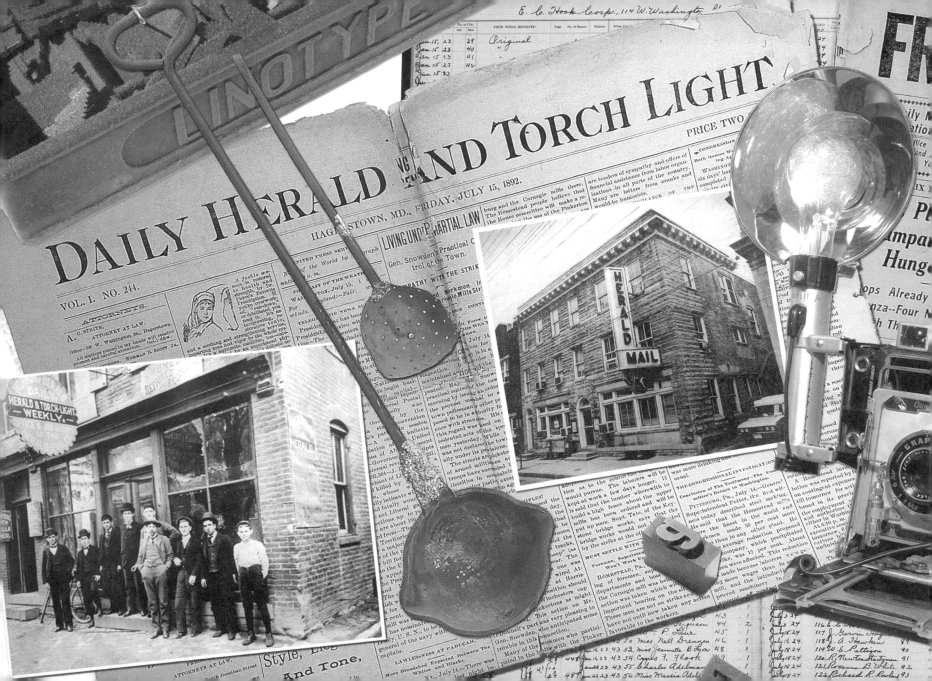